Side by Side

Side

Side

Exploring Your Neighborhood Through Intergenerational Activities

MIG Communications

Berkeley, California

A Curriculum Guide

by Matthew S. Kaplan

MIG Communications, 1802 Fifth Street, Berkeley, CA 94710, USA.
(510) 845-0953; fax (510) 845-8750

Originally published as *Neighborhoods 2000: An Intergenerational Urban Studies Curriculum*,
©1991 by the Bannon Group, New York, NY.

Printed in the United States of America.

Library of Congress Cataloging in Publication Data
Kaplan, Matthew S.
    Side by side : exploring your neighborhood through
intergenerational activities : a curriculum guide / Matthew S. Kaplan.
        p.   cm.
    Rev. ed. of: Neighborhoods - 2000. 1991.
    "Developed ... at the Center for Human Environments at the
Graduate School and University Center, City University of New York"-
-T.p. verso.
    Includes bibliographical references (p.   ).
    ISBN 0-944661-21-1
    1. Cities and towns--Study and teaching (Elementary)--United
States. 2. Neighborhood--Study and teaching (Elementary)--United
States. I. Kaplan, Matthew S. Neighborhoods - 2000. II. City
University of New York. Center for Human Environments. III. Title.
HT109.K28 1994
307.3'36316'0973--dc20   94-8908

Managing Editor: David Driskell
Assistant Editor: Julie Wildhaber
Illustrations: Melissa Mizell
Design: Tony Pierce, Anne Endrusick
Production Assistant: Christopher Hamilton
Copyeditor: Mi-Yung Rhee

The program of activities described in this book were developed by the author and his colleagues at the Center for Human
Environments at the Graduate School and University Center, City University of New York; and Hawaii Pacific University.

Additional support for program development was provided by the Mount Vernon Youth Bureau, Mount Vernon, New York.

Contents

Contents

Side by Side provides flexible guidelines for implementing an intergenerational program in which youth and senior adults work together to learn about their neighborhoods and about each other. The classroom and community activities were developed by my colleagues and me through extensive field projects. They represent an integrated, interdisciplinary curriculum that supports a number of educational goals. Activities are connected to subject areas in the academic curriculum, including social studies, civics, architecture and design, history, communications, and urban planning. Through program activities, participants learn key concepts and skills necessary for educational success and active citizenship, including teamwork, communication and planning skills, and critical thinking for defining and solving problems. The activities are geared primarily for use by teachers of fourth grade through junior high school classes and by community-based organizations interested in developing intergenerational programs.

The activities are based on projects conducted in New York State (in Mount Vernon, Long Island City, and East Harlem) and Hawaii (in downtown Honolulu, Ala Wai, Ewa, and Waikiki) between 1987 and 1993. These projects were organized and implemented under a program called *Neighborhoods–2000*, which I initiated at the City University of New York. The purpose of these original program efforts was to merge elements from the fields of urban environmental education and intergenerational programming into one interdisciplinary curriculum.

The book does not intend to prescribe a rigid curriculum but rather to provide a framework for schools and community centers to promote youth awareness of, and involvement in, neighborhood affairs. The senior adult volunteers, who come from the same neighborhoods as the youth participants, act as the catalyst for community education and action. While exploring their neighborhood, participants learn about each other and how to work together to effect change.

As an environmental psychologist, I am concerned with the loneliness, stress, and sense of alienation that many people experience in their everyday lives. My task is to develop ways to bring people together in meaningful, mutually supportive ways that enhance their control over their lives. Since I began experimenting with the program model seven years ago, I have been amazed at its potential for generating critical reflection and discussion about the psychological, social, and physical dimensions of community living and development. Each program reveals new possibilities for establishing the vital, community-building interpersonal relationships that determine our quality of life.

Acknowledgments

Although the program model presented in this book was originally developed by the Center for Human Environments at the City University of New York (CUNY) Graduate Center, recognition must also be given to those sponsoring organizations that launched the preliminary projects:

- *Downtown–2000* (Honolulu, 1991 to present), *Ala Wai–2000* (1992 to present), *Ewa–2000* (1992 to present), and *Waikiki–2000,* all sponsored by Hawaii Pacific University and the State of Hawaii Department of Education, with funding from the Gwenfread Allen Fund, the George P. and Ida Tenney Castle Trust, and the Wallace Alexander Gerbode Foundation;

- *Mount Vernon–2000* (1988 to present), sponsored by the Mount Vernon Youth Bureau, the Mount Vernon Council of Community Services, and the Mount Vernon Board of Education;

- *East Harlem–2000* (1989-1990), sponsored by the Union Settlement Association and a private funding source; and

- *Long Island City–2000* (1987-1988), sponsored by the New York City Youth Bureau and the New York City Board of Education.

I would also like to extend my sincere thanks to the key planners and supporters for each project. Their efforts and successes gave me the inspiration to continue developing the program and, ultimately, this book.

- *Downtown Honolulu, Ala Wai, Ewa,* and *Waikiki* (Hawaii): Chatt G. Wright, President, L. Jim Hochberg, Senior Vice President, Dr. Al Castle, Vice President for Development, Dr. John Fleckles, Academic Vice President, Dr. Leslie Correa, Academic Dean, and Caryl Corsi, Editorial Assistant, Hawaii Pacific University; Rachel Toh Alsagoff, Veronica Balsa, Shelli Bruder, Eugene Cabana, Magnus Englander, Gilbert Githere, Martha Heiligenmann, Janelle Kenny, Lei Lavarias, Sunardi Li, Doreen Ti, Kristy Hochberg, Jodi Oehlerking, Mary Ortel, Layle Watkins, and Ann Koh, Hawaii Pacific University student interns; Winchell Lee, Principal of Royal School; Irene Nakamoto, Principal of Ewa School; Judith Saranchok, Principal of Ala Wai School; Doris Choi, Principal of Waikiki School; Dr. Herman M. Aizawa, Acting Superintendent, State of Hawaii Department of Education; Meriel Collins, Director of the Seniors Actively Volunteering in Education program.

- *Mount Vernon* (Westchester, New York): Mayor Ronald A. Blackwood; Sioux Taylor, Commissioner of Recreation; Marlene Furtick, Executive Director of the Mount Vernon Youth Bureau; Dr. William

Prattella, District Superintendent for the Mount Vernon Board of Education; Bill Wertheim, Intergenerational Program Consultant; Lavinia B. Smith, Project Director; State Senator Suzi Oppenheimer; State Assemblyman Greg Young; Elizabeth Marrinan, Planning Consultant with the Mount Vernon Community Development Department; Marlene Wertheim, Mount Vernon Council of Community Services; Ruth Levister, Director of the Mount Vernon Office for the Aging; Diane Booker, Westchester Office of the Aging; Sal Quaranta, Director of the Mount Vernon Chamber of Commerce; Sandi Britton, Director of Westchester RSVP; and Donna Simpkins, Marymount College-Manhattan intern.

- *East Harlem* (New York, New York): Eugene Sklar, Executive Director of the Union Settlement Association; Joanne Gray, Director of the Washington Houses Community Center (WHCC); Jeff Holtzman, Director of Youth Services at WHCC; Reinaldo Martin, Director of Senior Services for the Union Settlement Association; Matilda Alvarez, Coordinator of Senior Services at WHCC; Lorie Novak, faculty member of the Photography Department at New York University; Meryl Levin and David Mager, New York University interns, Photography Department; Stacy Burow, WHCC staff person; and Mary Ester Malloy and Terry Maroney, volunteers.

- *Long Island City* (Queens, New York): Dr. Angelo Gimondo, Community Superintendent, School District #30, New York City Board of Education; Andrea Pack, Supervisor of Early Childhood, School District #30; Bea Flaig, Coordinator of Education in Human Values for School District #30; Philip Zemmel, Principal, P. S. 76; Marcia Cohen, District Coordinator, New York City School Volunteer Program; Rex Curry, Associate Director of the Pratt Institute Center for Environmental and Economic Development; Bob Disch, Brookdale Center for the Aging, Hunter College; Sunela Jayewardene, Pratt Institute intern, Architecture Department; Gloria Lisa Garcia, Queens College intern, Urban Studies Department; and James McDonald and Judy Jackson, Long Island City Interblock Association.

In addition to those involved with each project, the contributions of previous Center for Human Environments projects must be recognized. In particular, the Local Environmental Exploration and Exchange Project (1978-1980), funded by the U.S. Office of Environmental Education and conducted by Dr. Roger Hart, Cecilia Perez, and Cynthia Batterson, influenced the development of the program concepts and activities.

Special recognition must also be given to those individuals who served as "curriculum reviewers." They provided valuable input for the first edition of this guide:

- Lloyd Bromberg, Acting Director of Social Studies, New York City Board of Education

- Susan Edgar, Executive Director, New York City School Volunteer Program

- Helen Hamlin, Project Coordinator, Institute on Aging, School of Social Work, Columbia University

- Elizabeth Marrinan, Planning Consultant, Department of Planning and Community Development, Mount Vernon, New York

- Kathy Morin, Curriculum Development Consultant

- Andrea Pack, Supervisor of Early Childhood, Community School District #30, New York City Board of Education

- Janice Rao, Director of Elementary Schools, Mount Vernon Board of Education

- Andrea Sherman, Project Director, Elders Share the Arts

- Sioux Taylor, Commissioner of Recreation, Mount Vernon

Lastly, special thanks to those individuals who helped transform the ideas and experiences of these programs into this book's first edition: Kim Blakely, Ph.D., Research Associate at the Center for Human Environments, City University of New York Graduate Center; Roger Hart, Ph.D., Professor in the Ph.D. Program in Environmental Psychology and Director of the Center for Human Environments at the City University of New York Graduate Center; Bill Wertheim, Intergenerational Program Consultant in Mount Vernon, NY; Selim Iltus, Ph.D., of the Children's Environments Research Group, City University of New York Graduate Center; and Melissa Mizell, intern at the School of Art and Design at the Pratt Institute.

1

Welcome to *Side by Side*

he structure of today's living, learning, and recreation activities separate people according to age. As a result, youth and senior adults share neighborhoods but live in different worlds. This limits the opportunities for contact between generations and the potential benefits that might result.

At the same time, both youth and seniors depend on the local environment because of their limited mobility. The quality of their neighborhoods has a profound impact on the quality of their lives. Unfortunately, both groups are rarely in positions to effect change in their communities. Generally, they are not politically organized around local issues, are not in positions of decision-making power, and have limited resources with which to work.

Side by Side is a program of activities designed to help youth and senior adults have input into what their neighborhoods will look like in the future. It is also an educational curriculum that captures the interest of young people. As students look more closely at the world around them, they not only learn about their neighbors and their community, but they also learn a number of skills and disciplines.

Side by Side is:

- **Intergenerational.** Local senior adults are a valuable—and inexpensive—education resource. They help teachers coordinate the program activities and add an important dimension to classroom discussions, providing a direct link with the community-at-large as well as the community's past. The intergenerational learning—students and senior adults learning about and from each other—is a critical program dimension.

- **Interdisciplinary.** Examination and analysis of the local community provides a wide array of activities that draw on virtually every curriculum subject: writing, reading, communications, history, civics, art and architecture, urban studies, sociology, geology, and economics. The activities in this book provide many ideas that can be adapted and expanded to meet the needs of virtually any curriculum.

- **Relevant to People's Lives.** Young people enjoy discussing the world in which they live, particularly when it is as familiar as their own neighborhood. Students can spend hours examining a map of their neighborhood and developing ideas about potential improvements. *Side by Side* channels this enthusiasm through activities that emphasize skill development and knowledge attainment, resulting in educational experiences children will remember for years to come.

Program Goals

Most *Side by Side* activities are conducted in small intergenerational groups in which youth and senior adults discuss, evaluate, and present their ideas about community planning and living issues. The desired outcome is that they learn from each other and use this program as a means for sharing their perspectives with those responsible for making local development decisions.

The program strives to help participants:

- Learn about each other and from each other.

- Develop a greater understanding of their neighborhood and its users.

- Develop analytical, interpersonal, and presentation skills.

- Attain new knowledge in a wide range of academic disciplines.

- Achieve awareness of community planning dynamics and the value of individual participation in the community planning process.

The program is designed to support school-based learning. It uses the local environment as the medium for exploring a wide variety of subjects. Furthermore, depending on the background and past experience of the participants, strong multicultural themes can be woven into most of the program activities, helping educate participants about the heritage of their neighbors and of the neighborhood.

As a local studies initiative, the program promotes a view of citizenship in which the individual is an active participant in local issues. At a minimum, participants should learn that their neighborhoods are greatly affected by human action, that they have responsibility toward their neighborhoods, and that they have the potential to improve their neighborhoods through and beyond this program. Upon completion, the program can be used to generate a community forum in which participants present their concerns and advocate for desired changes to other residents, community planners, and decision makers.

A Team Approach

Side by Side requires a team approach. Because it is a community studies curriculum, it is important that the team of people who organize and implement the program have connections with the community-at-large. The best programs are those that have active support and participation from a wide range of people. While it may take some effort to organize the core group of people who will comprise the program team, it will be time well spent. As enthusiasm for the program grows and spreads, the role of the teacher or program leader can be more closely focused on classroom activities, while other team members coordinate resources and community-based activities.

Side by Side *requires a team approach to ensure a successful program that draws on community resources.*

Depending on the context, the program team might involve:

- Teachers and program leaders;

- Administrators from the school, school district, community center, or other sponsoring organization;

- Interns and other resource people from local colleges and universities;

- Representatives from potential co-sponsoring organizations, such as a local history organization, seniors group, or local government;

- Interested parents or grandparents who can contribute to the organization and coordination of program activities;

- A designated liaison from the group of senior adult volunteers participating in the program; and

- A youth representative from a local club or community service program.

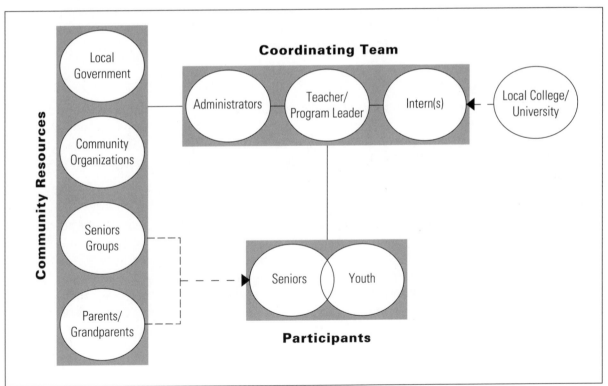

Structure of This Guide

This guide is organized in five sections:

I. Welcome to *Side by Side*

This section provides an overview of the program's philosophy and overall structure.

II. Program Start-Up

This section describes the preparation steps that must be completed before implementing *Side by Side*, including program planning, intern recruitment, and recruitment and training of senior adult volunteers.

III. Program Activities

This section presents the complete sequence of program activities and key considerations for implementing them. Activities are organized in nine "units." These units can be used either as a total curriculum or individually as special study segments. Each unit is described in six parts: Objectives; Concepts and Skills; Support Materials; Description of Activities; Homework Ideas; and Considerations.

IV. Additional Activity Ideas

In addition to providing a specific curriculum of activities, *Side by Side* encourages educators to develop their own activities based on the program's concept of promoting intergenerational interaction and exploring neighborhood living issues and concerns. This section presents ideas for additional activities that can be used to meet the special needs of different types of programs, such as after-school programs, summer recreation programs, etc.

V. Program Assessment

Because some *Side by Side* programs might emerge as multi-year endeavors, an evaluation component is useful for guiding ongoing program development and expansion. At the very least, participating youth and senior adult volunteers should fill out questionnaires or be interviewed before and after their involvement. Examples of pre- and post-program questionnaires are provided at the end of the book (see "Worksheets and Handouts" in the appendix). The program assessment section also presents strategies for documenting program events and determining whether objectives are being met.

Throughout the book—in boxes, appendices, and worksheets—there are resource materials designed to assist in implementing, publicizing, and evaluating *Side by Side* programs. These materials include: program development ideas and activities, recruitment strategies, homework ideas, questionnaires, and permission and weekly log forms. Additional program resources are referenced in "Contacts" (page 89).

Program Start-up

Organize the Program Team

A successful program requires planning and preparation well in advance of program implementation. This section covers a number of the issues that must be addressed during the program start-up period. If the complete program of activities presented in this book are to be implemented, a start-up period of at least eight weeks should be allowed (see page 14).

The first step in the program planning process is to organize the team of people who will oversee the program's planning and implementation. Members of the program coordinating team will be responsible for helping recruit interns and senior adult volunteers and will assist in obtaining resource materials, developing community contacts, and coordinating program activities.

The program coordinating team should include:

- The teacher or program leader, interns, and others who will work directly with the students and senior adult volunteers in implementing the program activities.

- Administrators from the sponsoring organization (school, community center, youth program).

- Representatives from relevant local community organizations, such as a local history organization or agency of the local government who can co-sponsor and help coordinate program activities.

- Interested parents or grandparents of students participating in the program who can help establish community connections and coordinate program activities.

The roles and responsibilities of each team member must be clearly defined and the tasks and timelines for program implementation set forth. Roles and responsibilities may be defined in whatever manner makes sense based on the composition of the coordinating team and the program of activities being undertaken. However, there are two roles that are critical to every coordinating team:

- *A designated contact person for the senior adult volunteers.* This individual maintains close contact with the senior adult volunteers and keeps them informed regarding program activities and schedules. He or she should also assist with logistical issues related to the participation of senior adult volunteers, such as transportation to and from the program site and training activities prior to the start of the program.

The coordinating team is
critical to the planning
and implementation of
Side by Side.

- *An administrative person responsible for program coordination.* This individual will help oversee program planning and implementation functions. While he or she will not necessarily be responsible for actual implementation of such functions, it will be this person's responsibility to coordinate program schedules, assign tasks to team members, and ensure that all program activities are properly planned and implemented. The tasks for which this person will be responsible include:

  — Working with local colleges to obtain interns.

  — Resolving logistical issues, such as making provisions for a quiet meeting space.

  — Coordinating the use of available resources, such as school facilities, a local library, or a computer center.

  — Recruiting, arranging for training of, and providing recognition for senior adult volunteers. These activities might involve coordinating with city, state, and federal organizations that promote and support senior volunteerism.

  — Obtaining resource materials for mapping, model-building, interviewing, photography, and other activities.

  — Contacting community-based organizations and city agencies to develop ways in which they might assist program participants in exploring local issues.

  — Helping to publicize the program in the local media.

Identify Activities

The first task of the program coordinating team will be to develop the program of activities to be undertaken. The program of activities presented in this book is recommended, but it may be easily adapted to meet the particular needs of specific programs and settings. A condensed version of *Side by Side* can be implemented over the course of a week (for example, as a special unit in a summer program) or a tailored version of the program can be conducted to tie its activities more closely to a school's ongoing curriculum structure over the course of the school year.

To develop the program of activities, review the sections in this book titled "Program Activities" and "Additional Activity Ideas." Then, consider the time and resources available to your program and the extent of commitment that can be expected. Be realistic, but at the same time, remember that a program like *Side by Side* generates enthusiasm among its participants. Limited resources can go a long way when people get involved and have a stake in the program's success.

The graphic below illustrates the recommended program of activities for *Side by Side*.

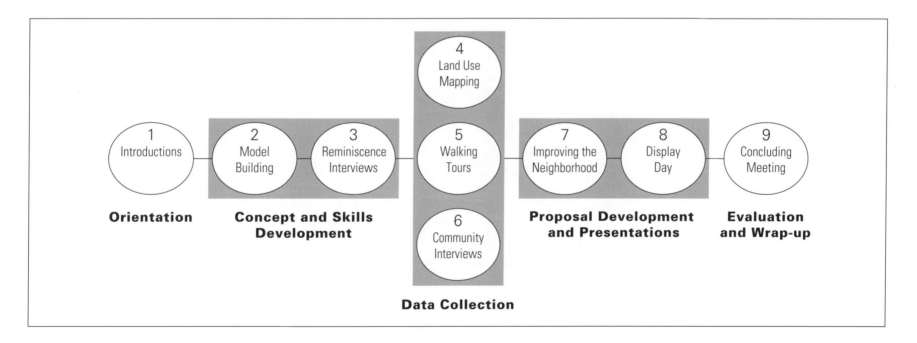

Develop the Timeline

The complete sequence of activities should be mapped on a calendar to ensure that adequate time has been allotted for each. Based on the experience of other projects, the following time allotments are needed to complete the activities outlined in this book:

- **Program Start-up:** 8 weeks

- **Program Implementation:** 24 weeks

- **Post-Program Evaluation:** 4 weeks

This timeline should be modified according to the particular needs and schedule of each program. Since each program creates its own tempo, a certain amount of flexibility in scheduling is needed. The number of sessions allotted for each activity will vary depending on the skill and interest level of the youth and senior adult participants, and schedules will need to bend to accommodate the logistics of planning and conducting the field-intensive activities (i.e., the community interviews and walking tours).

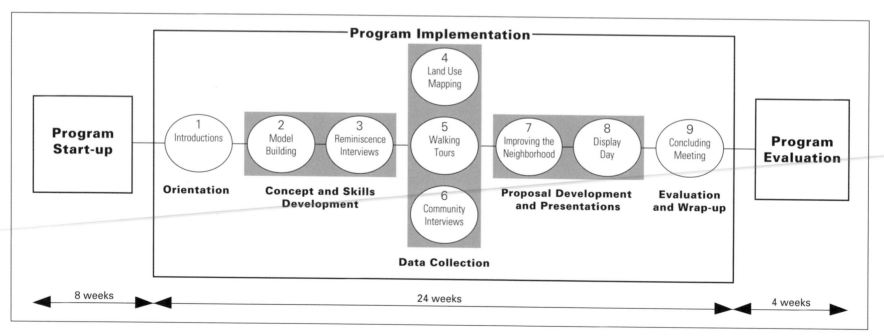

INTERNSHIP OPPORTUNITY!

Side by Side
Intergenerational Neighborhood Studies Program

Side by Side is an innovative intergenerational program at _____ that brings local youth and senior adults together to explore and address neighborhood concerns. One to three interns are needed to work on this program from _____ to _____ for a total of _____ hours each week.

Interns will help develop, conduct, and evaluate a series of activities, including: land use mapping, model building, neighborhood walking tours, community interviews, photographic surveys, community needs assessments, and development and presentation of neighborhood improvement ideas.

Individual interns may focus on one or more of the following program components:

- **Activities Development**—identifying community resources and developing program materials and neighborhood-based learning activities.

- **Group Facilitation**—working with intergenerational groups to discuss local history and current planning issues.

- **Program Planning and Evaluation**—performing various assessments to identify the program's strengths and weaknesses and its impact on students, senior adults, and local government.

Program participants will meet at _____, located at _____, from _____ to _____ each week.

For more information, contact _____.

A flyer like this can be posted at a local college or university to attract potential interns.

Probably the most important step for ensuring adequate curriculum support is to recruit one to three undergraduate or graduate students from local colleges. College interns can help: identify community resources, develop program materials, plan activities, meet weekly with the senior adults, facilitate communication and cooperation between youth and seniors, establish community linkages that will enrich the fieldwork activities, and assess and document program impact on participants.

Side by Side can be used to fulfill fieldwork requirements or provide internship credits for students from a variety of fields, including: gerontology, psychology, sociology, geography, urban studies, urban planning, architecture, history, education, film, and photography. Interns from any of these fields have much to gain in the form of credits, responsibility, and professional experience. A college intern recruitment flyer sent to the appropriate college personnel can help in recruiting interns and clarifying their program-related responsibilities (see sample at left).

If interns are not available, you may be able to find parents who would be interested in performing some of these functions. It is also possible that one or more of the senior adult volunteers might be retired from jobs such as teaching that have provided them with experience in these areas.

Recruit and Train Volunteers

Side by Side can be implemented with as few as three and as many as eleven senior adult volunteers. Seniors can be recruited through:

- Local senior citizen groups.

- Citywide or county senior volunteer programs.

- Publicity in local newspapers (see following page).

- Open houses introducing the program, conducted at least four weeks before the program begins.

- Distribution of a recruitment flyer throughout the neighborhood, targeting senior citizen centers and other places seniors frequent.

- Word of mouth.

- Contacting youth participants' older relatives.

Another approach to senior volunteer recruitment is planning short-term events in which prospective volunteers have a chance to meet and interact with youth before making a commitment to a longer program. For example, a program in Mount Vernon, New York, held an intergenerational event called "Dreams for the Future," which is described in the sample press release on page 27.

There are no requirements that senior adults need to fulfill before they can participate in the program. However, it does help if they have lived in the neighborhood for at least three years and display a sincere interest in working with youth. Because training will be provided by members of the coordinating team, past experience working with youth is not necessary.

Articles such as this in local papers are useful tools for recruiting senior adult volunteers.

The Mount Vernon Times

Voice of The City of Homes

Vol. 3 No. 44   Monday, October 30, 1989

Mount Vernon - 2000 Seeking Volunteers

Last year, students from Washington School and a group of senior citizen volunteers worked together to explore Mount Vernon's past and present and to try to figure out what it will look like in the Year 2000.

Participating youth and senior citizens met every Tuesday morning to learn from each other's experiences and examine important community issues. Activities included: model building of the 'ideal' neighborhood; reminiscence exercises where seniors recounted their community memories and experiences; tours of neighborhood facilities; creative writing about neighborhood issues; and land use mapping and photographic neighborhood surveys.

This year, "Mount Vernon - 2000", a Mount Vernon Youth Bureau sponsored project, will be expanded to involve two classes of Washington School students. Therefore, several openings are now available for senior citizens (over 60 years old) who are interested in volun-

teering for this project. The only requirements are a general familiarity with the "southside" of Mount Vernon and a sincere interest for working with children. Since training will be provided, past experience working with children is not necessary.

Volunteers will work with the students every Thursday morning or afternoon, from December to June. The first meeting will take place on November 9th at City Hall. If you are interested or want further information, call either Matt Kaplan at 212-876-8524 or Bill Wertheim at 664-5681. Mr. Kaplan and Mr. Wertheim are co-directors of the project, and they request that calls be made before November 7.

The "Mount Vernon - 2000" project model was originally developed by the Center for Human Environments at the City University of New York Graduate Center. This project was launched last year by the Mount Vernon Youth

Bureau and the Mount Vernon Council of Community Services. Some funding assistance was provided by the Mount Vernon Chamber of Commerce and the Westchester Youth Bureau, and a New York State legislative grant is forthcoming through the auspices of Senator Suzi Oppenheimer and Assemblyman Greg Young.

Training Session for Senior Adult Volunteers

December 9, 1988
Washington School

Introduction and Overview
9:00 - 9:30
Matt Kaplan, Project Co-Director

What Are Schools Like Today?
What Are They Trying to Accomplish?
9:30 - 10:00
Nellie Thornton, Principal, Washington School
Greg McDonald, Teacher, Class 6-M

Discovering Mount Vernon's Resources
Marlene Wertheim, Subcommittee on the Elderly,
10:00 - 10:15
Mount Vernon Council of Community Services

Planning, Zoning, and Citizen Participation
Liz Marrinan, Community Development Dept.
10:15 - 10:30
City of Mount Vernon

What Are Intergenerational Programs?
How Do Children Typically View Older People?
10:30 - 10:50
Bill Wertheim, Co-Director, Mount Vernon-2000

Senior Adult Volunteers as Resources
Volunteers interview each other in pairs and, as a group,
10:50 - 11:25
discuss possible connections with the students and school.

Wrap-up
11:25 - 11:35

The agenda above provides an example of the items to include in the preliminary training session for senior adult volunteers.

Members of the coordinating team have a vital role to play in clarifying an appropriate training agenda. Basic training for senior adult volunteers should consist of a pre-program seminar and ongoing pre- and post-activity meetings in which seniors:

- Examine program objectives;

- Learn about how schools and community centers have changed in the past couple generations;

- Review strategies for working with youth;

- Learn how community development decisions are made; and

- Plan subsequent activities.

An important goal of the preliminary meetings is to create an atmosphere of mutual assistance among the senior adults. The camaraderie developed in these meetings can help ensure continued involvement in the program. To this end, you may wish to consult the *Seniors Teaching Seniors* manual developed by the Institute on Aging at Columbia University (Stuen et al., 1982).

Develop Community Connections

Each *Side by Side* program will have its own character. It will reflect the educational philosophy, values, and priorities of the sponsoring organization and group members. However, one significant feature of all programs will be the frequent and consistent use of the local neighborhood, its people, and its resources.

It is critical that a strong relationship with the community be established early in the evolution of each program. For school-based programs, a good school-community bond will greatly enhance the curriculum and provide participating teachers, students, and senior adult volunteers with additional learning resources.

The families of program participants can also be a valuable resource. Be sure to request feedback from parents, grandparents, and other family members regarding resources they may be able to offer and whether they would be willing to join in the walking tours or help out with other program activities.

Side by Side should also establish connections to other organizations in the community. City agency representatives, local politicians, community group leaders, and other interested residents involved in the various program activities should be invited to visit the program site to meet with the participants and engage in continued discussion and debate. These links are critical for enhancing participants' learning of and involvement in local development dynamics. Developing these connections will require a series of meetings between members of the coordinating team and representatives of community agencies. These meetings can be used to develop strategies for integrating community resources into the program.

Some important places to contact are:

- Community centers and clubs for youth and senior adults

- Local schools

- City agencies and local planning boards

- The mayor's office (particularly in small cities and towns)

- Police precincts

- Local libraries

- Hospitals

- Parks

- Merchants and merchant associations

- Local historical associations

- Fire departments

- Religious centers

- Chambers of commerce

- Environmental improvement groups such as garden clubs and other neighborhood beautification groups

There are a number of resources that can be consulted for guidance on how to organize community resources to support a curriculum like *Side by Side*. These include Ward and Fyson (1973); Hart (1987); Baldassari, Lehman, and Wolfe (1987); and the *Training Student Organizers' Curriculum* developed by the Council on the Environment of New York City and written by Zamm, Ortner, and DeAngelis (1990). The Council on the Environment curriculum describes various community organization projects with youth groups, from anti-litter drives to letter-writing campaigns expressing concern about the transportation of nuclear wastes.

Side by Side can become a community-wide effort through special events such as the "Dreams for the Future" festivals held in Long Island City and Mount Vernon. These events were organized by community organizations, with the participation of local schools, as a means of bringing neighborhood residents together to create and display models, murals, and other exhibits that depicted popular images and ideas for future neighborhood development. The press release from the Mount Vernon festival is shown on page 27 as an example of how such an event might be publicized to community residents. For more information about intergenerational special events, see Kaplan (1990).

The most important materials to obtain before the program begins are:

- Personal journals (blank books) for all of the participants.

- Neighborhood maps and aerial photographs, available from city planning departments and sometimes from community advisory boards or other organizational bodies that coordinate and improve city services.

- Diverse arts, crafts, and graphics supplies, many of which can be collected or recycled from home. These include model-building supplies, such as 3' x 3' (or longer) cardboard bases, poster paper, construction paper, pipe cleaners, cotton balls, aluminum foil, various textile materials, glitter, glue, and tape.

For the land use mapping unit, the following are needed:

- Outline maps (6-8 copies)

- Land use maps and/or aerial photographs (1-2 copies)

- Colored pencils (5 sets of 10-12 colors)

- Colored stickers or push pins

Most of the materials and supplies listed above—with the exception of the maps—are easy to find at low cost. Cameras and tape recorders are also desirable but are not essential for the program.

Program Activities

The sequence of program units presented on the following pages is recommended to provide a complete and coherent structure for your *Side by Side* program. However, these units may be easily adapted to meet the particular needs of specific programs and settings, as discussed in the previous section. If you choose to adapt the program, be sure to review the "Additional Activity Ideas" (Section IV) as well as the activities presented in this section.

The nine units and related activities presented in this section are:

Unit 1   Introductions

Unit 2   Model Building

Unit 3   Reminiscence Interviews

Unit 4   Land-Use Mapping

Unit 5   Walking Tours

Unit 6   Community Interviews

Unit 7   Improving the Neighborhood

Unit 8   Display Day

Unit 9   Concluding Meeting

Each unit is presented in six parts: Objectives; Concepts and Skills; Support Materials; Description of Activities; Homework Ideas; and Considerations. In addition, several overall considerations are presented on the following two pages.

Overall Considerations

Program leaders should keep the following considerations in mind when implementing *Side by Side* activities:

- **Integration with the General Curriculum**
  There are many potential connections between the activities described in this book and the basic or "core" curriculums administered by many schools. Each *Side by Side* unit includes a "Concepts and Skills" section describing key concepts and academic skills learned in the activities and, where appropriate, relationships to school subjects. Each unit also includes homework ideas. To make the most of potential connections to the general curriculum, program leaders may:

  — Assign creative writing assignments related to the different activities.

  — Actively involve auxiliary educational personnel in program activities (e.g., art teachers, audio-visual personnel, librarians).

  — Incorporate elements of the general curriculum into program activities. For example, earth science lessons related to environmental issues can be woven into the "Walk-About, Talk-About" activity described in Unit 5.

  — Use the journal as a tool for learning (see below).

- **Journal Keeping**
  An effective way to promote personal reflection on the ideas and experiences of *Side by Side* is to encourage students and senior adults to keep personal journals. The handout titled "My Journal and Me" at the end of this book (see "Worksheets and Handouts") can be used to encourage program participants to keep personal journals for recording:

  — Perceptions of program activities.

  — Attitudes toward each other.

  — Neighborhood attachments; i.e., identifying and describing places which have personal importance.

  — Places they feel pose a problem that should be improved in the future.

  — Experiences related to neighborhood problems, such as pollution, drugs, or crime.

Publicity in local newspapers and other media provides valuable recognition for the efforts and ideas of program participants. It can also help make their concerns a legitimate part of a community dialogue regarding local development issues.

The easiest way to reach the local media is to develop and distribute a press release. The sample press release on this page announced a pre-program event in Mount Vernon. With luck, local newspapers will send a photographer and a reporter or ask the group to submit photos and a story. In either case, parental permission will be necessary to photograph (or videotape) students for publicity purposes. A parental permission form is provided at the end of this book (see "Worksheets and Handouts"). It might also be prudent to obtain the permission of the senior adults for use of their pictures, names, and stories for publicity purposes.

Another strategy for notifying the public about the program is to keep bulletin boards devoted to program-related information in visible locations at the host school or community center, participating seniors organizations, and other community-based organizations. Periodic updates can also be sent to local churches and synagogues for inclusion in their weekly bulletins.

*A press release such as this can be sent to local media to request coverage of **Side by Side** events.*

FOR IMMEDIATE RELEASE

Contact: P.R. King
798-6671

Request for Coverage

Event: Mount Vernon "Dreams for the Future" Festival
Date: August 12, 1989
Time: 11:00 am to 4:00 pm
Place: Hartley Park; Playground Area

The "Dreams for the Future Festival," sponsored by the Mount Vernon Youth Bureau, will be a day-long look at the Year 2000 in Westchester's southernmost city. The event is designed to give people who live and work in Mount Vernon a chance to share their thoughts and concerns about the city's future.

All community groups and organizations have been invited to develop displays, presentations, and workshops that will help promote civic awareness and communication about life in Mount Vernon.

A ceremonial tree planting will commemorate the festival. Also planned is an intergenerational bocce tournament, a puppet show on recycling, and a children's workshop. Highlighting the day will be a performance by the Mount Vernon High School Black Unity Gospel Choir. A group of Mount Vernon teens has also organized a set of performances. The Mount Vernon Department of Planning and Community Development will display sketches of several new buildings and other projects now under way.

Everyone who cares about Mount Vernon is invited to participate!

Background: The festival is being held as part of the Mount Vernon–2000 project in which local senior citizen volunteers join elementary school students in exploring local planning issues. For the second consecutive year, the project will operate out of the Washington School beginning in the Fall.

###

UNIT 1: Introductions

Objectives

- To introduce participants to the program and to each other.

- To help participants identify age-related issues and stereotypes.

Concepts and Skills

- **Concepts:** Clarifying perceptions of aging; identifying ageism and age-related stereotypes in literature and popular culture; developing heightened awareness of how misconceptions are developed.

- **Academic Skills Enhanced:** Articulation of personal experience and social observation in verbal and written forms.

Support Materials

- Chart paper or blackboard *(for all activities)*

- Nametags *(for all activities)*

- Program Overview Chart, as a handout or as a large display *(for activity 1B)*

- Journals *(for activity 1B)*

- "My Journal and Me" handouts *(for activity 1B)*

- "Getting to Know You" interview questionnaires *(for activity 1D)*

- Two bags of M&Ms™ *(for activity 1E)*

- *Optional*—Books or films with intergenerational themes, such as *On Golden Pond* or *The Best of You . . . The Best of Me* (Generations Together 1986)

- *Optional*—Photos of people of different ages involved in joint activities.

Activity 1A: Preliminary Meetings

If time permits, meet with the program participants in youth-only and senior adults-only groups prior to the first intergenerational group meeting to discuss age-related perceptions. Questions that might be posed at these meetings include:

- How old is a senior adult/young person?

- What do they look like?

- What do you think senior adults/youth like to do for fun?

- What do they feel like when they go to the store? take the bus? go to the park? exercise?

- Do you think senior adults/youth feel the same way about the neighborhood as you do? What do you think their main concerns are?

- What are some of the problems in your neighborhood that concern youth and not senior adults? That concern senior adults and not youth?

- Where do we see youth in the neighborhood and where not? Where do we see seniors in the neighborhood and where not?

List responses to these questions on a blackboard or on chart paper to serve as a beginning point for the first intergenerational group discussion (see Activity 1B) and as a record of initial perceptions to be reviewed at later points in the program.

Activity 1B: Orientation

This activity should be conducted at the first intergenerational meeting of the program participants. Members of the program coordinating team should do their best to create a friendly and relaxed atmosphere.

Following a brief welcome and introductions, the program coordinator should provide an orientation to *Side by Side* and help participants understand the structure and magnitude of the program they are about to experience. The program overview (see page 13) can be distributed in a handout and/or presented on a large display board to illustrate the program's structure.

The orientation discussion should include:

- Review of age-related stereotypes, including those raised in the preliminary single generation meetings.

- Overview of the program's activities and goals.

- Review of expectations that participants will function as community co-investigators and activists.

- Emphasis on the value of each participant keeping a journal to record impressions throughout the program (use the "My Journal and Me" handout—included at the end of this book—to introduce journal-writing expectations).

Once this discussion is completed, activities 1C through 1H can be used to help introduce participants to each other and to further explore (and break down) age-related stereotypes.

Activity 1C: "Age-Line" Exercise

The "Age-Line" exercise is an excellent way to elicit participants' perceptions about aging and to stimulate dialogue about age-related issues among group members.

- To begin, program participants and staff (including the coordinator, interns, and visitors) place themselves in a line from the youngest to the oldest member of the group. (This may also be done in a circle.) Everybody looks around. Discuss how it feels to be that age (self-conscious, happy, frustrated, etc.). Create age categories on chart paper and write down the feelings expressed.

- Now program participants and staff line up according to their *desired* age. Everyone then takes turns stating why they chose the age they did. Ask what it means to be that age and what they think they could do at that age that they can't do now.

The "Getting to Know You" interview provides a structure for intergenerational introductions.

Activity 1D: "Getting to Know You" Interviews

This activity encourages interaction between group members and, as the title suggests, helps people get to know each other better.

- Organize participants in small groups (one senior adult volunteer to a group), mixing participants so that each group contains young people from a variety of neighborhoods.

- Pass out the "Getting to Know You" interview questionnaire (see "Worksheets and Handouts" at the end of the book) and ask participants to conduct interviews with each other. Depending on the time available, groups might break into pairs for the interviews or the group as a whole might interview every individual in the group.

Activity 1E: The M&Ms™ Game

This game is a good ice-breaker, providing a snack while helping participants get to know one another better.

- Using the same groups formed for the "Getting to Know You" interviews, give a bag or bowl of M&Ms to each group.

- Ask participants to take turns selecting M&Ms from the bag or bowl (without looking). For each M&M they choose, have them say something about how they feel about their neighborhood based on the color they choose:

Red	Say something that you dislike about your neighborhood.
Light Brown	Say something that you like about your neighborhood.
Green	Say something about what you like to do in your neighborhood.
Dark Brown	Say something about your neighborhood that you would like to change.
Orange	Say something about your neighborhood that you fear.
Yellow	Say something about the world that you would like to change.

Activity 1F: Growing Up, Growing Older

This activity encourages program participants to think critically about the stereotypes they have of other generations. It was developed by the Center for Understanding Aging in Framingham, MA (see "Contacts," page 89).

To begin the activity, the statements listed below should be written on a blackboard or large sheet of paper or they can be typed up and handed out.

1. *They always stick together and keep their distance from other age groups.*

2. *I hate the way they drive. They're a menace on the road.*

3. *They're always taking and never giving. They think the world owes them a living.*

4. *They're so opinionated. They think they know it all.*

5. *They're never satisfied, always complaining about something.*

6. *Don't hire them, you can't depend on them.*

7. *Don't they have anything better to do than hang around the parks and shopping malls?*

8. *Why are they always so forgetful?*

9. *I wish I had as much freedom as they have.*

10. *Why don't they act their age?*

Participants should then be given the following instructions:

- Each of the these statements expresses a stereotype about a group of people only defined as "they." Discuss each statement in terms of whether you think a younger person is talking about older people or an older person is talking about young people, and why.

- Which statements represent common stereotypes of young people? Of older people? Of both?

- Stereotypes are the basis for prejudice and discrimination. As a youth or an adult, have you ever experienced (or known anyone who experienced) prejudice or discrimination based on age (for example, when applying for a job, renting an apartment, or trying to participate in some activity of another age group)?

- Can both younger and older people be the victims of prejudice and discrimination based on age? Are there any other ways in which "growing up" is similar to "growing old?" What are they?

- What could and should be done about age-based prejudice and discrimination? Is this a problem that older and younger people could work on together?

Activity 1G: Greetings! (A Theatrical Ice-breaker)

This activity was developed by Elders Share the Arts, Inc., of Brooklyn, NY (see "Contacts," page 89). It is an effective ice-breaker and a dynamic way to begin intergenerational gatherings. It is recommended for beginning groups as a prelude to improvisational work. There are several variations. The basic greeting exercise asks two people (a young person and a senior adult) to greet each other in different ways.

- Two people stand back-to-back, a few feet apart from one another. The leader calls out different states of being, each time suggesting different greetings. For example:

    — Two old friends who meet suddenly after a long separation, overjoyed to see each other.

    — A meeting between two people who are angry.

    — A humorous meeting.

    — A meeting between two sad people.

    — A meeting between one person who is angry and one person who is afraid.

- When the direction is given, the two people turn and greet one another. When the meeting is over, they turn back around and wait for the next instruction.

- End the exercise by having people greet each other as they really are.

Participants can vary their greeting by saying it, singing it, screaming it, signing it, or mirroring each other's greetings. Participants who are frail can do this exercise by pretending the greeting is taking place on the telephone.

Activity 1H: Talk Show

This activity develops interview skills and helps participants get to know each other better.

- Before beginning the "talk show," have participants meet for 10 to 20 minutes to discuss the interview topics. This will provide interviewers with the necessary background material related to the life experiences of the interviewees. Topics might include:

  — How it feels to be a senior adult in your neighborhood.

  — How things have changed in your neighborhood over the past 10 (20, 30, 40) years.

  — How being a teenager today is different from being a teenager in the past.

  Ask interviewers to write their questions on 3" x 5" file cards (one question per card) and encourage use of different types of questions:

  — **Open-ended questions** to elicit a wide range of responses (e.g., "How does it feel to be interviewed?").

  — **Close-ended questions** that provide a more focused, specific response (e.g., "Do you think there should be more, the same amount, or fewer sanitation workers in your neighborhood?").

  — **Probing questions** that are generally open-ended but which follow up on earlier responses to obtain more information on a specific topic (e.g., "Why do you feel that way?" or "Can you expand on your last answer, please?").

- Talk show hosts can set the stage by (dramatically) stating the name of the show and introducing the participants (real or fictitious).

- Begin with a small group of young people interviewing a senior adult, or with one senior adult and one young person interviewing a group of young people. Set a time limit of 5 to 15 minutes for each interview, depending on the time available and the group size. Remember, the more "real" the talk show is, the more fun it becomes. Decorate the room like a TV studio, with the show's name on a large signboard. Play music and have commercial breaks. Ask participants to dress up and to bring in photos and other objects that identify themselves. Have fun!

Other Ideas

- **Physical Warm-Up Activities:**

  Physical activities can help people relax and raise the energy level and camaraderie of a group. These activities can also help participants learn about physical capabilities and the physiological changes associated with aging. Most physical activities can be modified so they can be done in a standing or sitting position.

  — *Dance/movement exercises.* These activities can be simple, such as holding hands and swaying to music, or more elaborate, such as square dancing with intergenerational partners. Keep in mind that the use of props and music from the different generations can help enliven these exercises.

  — *Physical exercises and basic stretches.* Seniors and youth can take turns conducting exercise sessions.

- **An Intergenerational Non-Stereotype Collage**

  For the first month of the program, youth and senior adult volunteers can bring in images of seniors, children, and teenagers engaged in non-stereotypical activities. Participants can bring both positive and negative examples from various media. These images are then placed on a large sheet of paper in the group meeting room, forming an evolving collage of non-stereotypical images. Youth can also draw pictures to add to the collection. The collage can involve themes related to how people look, how they feel, how and where they have fun, and how they typically spend their time. This collage should help reinforce participants' awareness of the age-related stereotypes they identify during other Unit 1 activities and convey the need for more positive age-related messages and images in the media.

Homework Ideas

The activities in Unit 1 provide a number of opportunities for creative homework assignments that can help develop writing skills, interview skills, observational skills, and knowledge of local history and the aging process.

- List the qualities that young people and senior adults have and write a paragraph about what it would be like to be a senior adult. Where would you live? Whom would you be with? What would your body look and feel like? How would you spend your time?

- Write a short paragraph about the oldest or youngest person you know. What do you know about him or her? What makes this person stay in your mind? Be sure to mention one special thing about this person that interests you.

- Interview a senior adult you know (a neighbor, a friend, a grandparent, a program participant). What was their neighborhood like when they were growing up? What did they do for fun? What was their school like? What important events were taking place in the world?

Considerations

Be sure to stress to participants that the program is a means of investigating important issues relevant to their lives. This subjective dimension makes the program more than a series of skills development exercises; it is an opportunity to explore issues and ideas that are important to them and applicable to their daily lives.

Objectives

- To stimulate youth and senior adult participants to experiment with neighborhood planning and design options.

- To encourage participants to discuss community "quality of life" issues such as recreational opportunities, vandalism, and safety.

- To function as an "ice-breaking" device between and within the generations and to reassure participants that they will determine what they develop in this program.

Concepts and Skills

- **Concepts:** Neighborhood and community; social services; democracy; community participation.

- **Academic Skills Enhanced:** Public speaking; interviewing; resourcefulness with materials; model building; planning; surveying; learning to work as part of a group.

Support Materials

Arts and crafts materials of different shapes, textures, and sizes should be collected from the school or community center and participants' homes at the beginning of the program. These items might include milk cartons, tin cans, plastic wrap, toilet tissue, fabric remnants, pipe cleaners, and ice cream sticks.

Activity 2A: Defining "Neighborhood"

Conduct a discussion with the entire group, encouraging active participation from the senior adult volunteers. The purpose of the discussion is to help participants understand that a "neighborhood" is the combination of many factors—people, buildings, institutions, social interaction, history, etc. The discussion should identify the important elements and the desired features of a neighborhood. Questions you might use to help focus the discussion include:

- What is a neighborhood?

- What do people need from a neighborhood?

- What is the ideal neighborhood?

The illustration on the facing page provides a graphic framework for defining "neighborhood." To get the youth thinking about their neighborhoods, the following language might help: "describe the areas around your home where you feel the most 'comfortable' or 'at home.'"

"NEIGHBORHOOD"

INSTITUTIONS and ORGANIZATIONS
PROVIDERS OF HEALTH RELATED, TRANSPORTATION, RECREATION, AND OTHER SERVICES

PSYCHOLOGICAL
LIKES AND DISLIKES; MEMORIES; NEEDS MET BY LOCAL ORGANIZATIONS.

COMMUNITY FAIR

PROSPECT BUS

HISTORICAL
EACH NEIGHBORHOOD HAS A UNIQUE SET OF HISTORICAL MEANINGS AND EVENTS

SOCIAL
PEOPLE DOING THINGS TOGETHER

POLLUTION PROBLEMS

PHYSICAL CHARACTER
SPATIAL BOUNDARIES; TYPES OF BUILDINGS; AMOUNT OF LITTER; ETC.

ATMOSPHERE
THE UNIQUE "FLAVOR" OR "FEEL" OF A NEIGHBORHOOD

Activity 2B: Design the Ideal Neighborhood

In this activity, groups of senior adults and youth build models of their "ideal" neighborhood. This requires group agreement on what constitutes an ideal neighborhood and cooperation in constructing a model of that neighborhood. Models can be simple or elaborate, literal or abstract. The process of building the model can be extremely engaging and a lot of fun. It also encourages group cooperation, exchange of ideas, and creative expression. Be sure to have a wide variety of materials on hand so that groups can wield their imaginations freely!

■   Organize participants into small working groups, with one senior adult and three to eight youth in each group.

Building a model of the "ideal neighborhood" provides a fun environment for group interaction and creativity.

■   Tell each group to review the important elements and desired features of a neighborhood that were identified in the large group discussion.

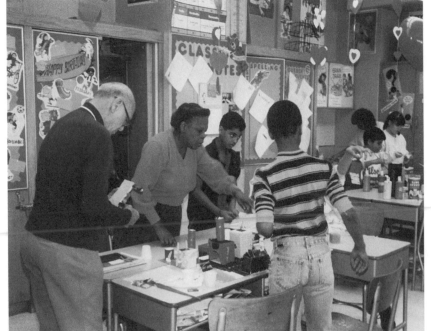

■   Each group should develop an overall approach for creating a model of their ideal neighborhood. Staff should assist groups in the development of their plans. For example, some groups might choose to work on one quadrant at a time; another might choose to first build residences, then recreational facilities, and so on.

■   Participants should feel free to utilize a wide range of materials, including various types of paper, cardboard, clay, crayons, markers, and any other materials they bring from home or have available for creating their ideal neighborhoods.

■   When the models are completed, groups make presentations and answer questions about their neighborhood plans and model-building processes. Emphasis should be placed on the community living concerns and goals that are implied by the physical configurations and features of each model.

Model building requires group decision making and teamwork.

Homework Ideas

- Bring in magazine pictures of other neighborhoods and write comparisons of these neighborhoods to your ideal neighborhood in terms of quality of life, residents, recreational facilities, availability of services, shopping areas, and other community concerns.

Considerations

Model building is a fun activity that will enable the youth and senior adults to get to know each other in a low-pressure environment. This activity also stimulates participants to develop their planning skills and to clarify their neighborhood concerns before meeting local planning and human service professionals in later phases of the program. Accordingly, in conducting this activity, the program coordinator should emphasize the importance of creativity and the possible implications for daily living of the participants' neighborhood designs. Be sure to save these models so that they can be exhibited on "Display Day" (see Unit 8, pages 70-72).

UNIT 3: Reminiscence Interviews

Objectives

- To teach youth and senior adults how to interview to elicit information from each other about their skills, knowledge, and experiences.

Concepts and Skills

- **Concepts:** Personal history; the family as a unit of life and study; history as a living, ongoing process; cultural diversity.

- **Academic Skills Enhanced:** Development and execution of a structured interview; familiarity with audio tape recording technology; understanding of historical events guiding people's lives over the last forty to seventy years; ability to recognize alternate perspectives; development of constructive attitudes toward diversity.

Support Materials

- Mini-tape recorders (one per group). These might be borrowed from school or community center audio-visual facilities, or local stores might be willing to donate supplies.

- Audio tapes (one per group).

- Two copies of each taped interview, one for the school or local library and one for the senior adult volunteers.

Activity 3A: Prepare for the Interview Process

To maximize the learning potential of this unit, some or all of the following exercises might be used to help prepare participants for the interview process:

- **Develop a historical timeline.** This is a useful group activity that will help youth develop interview questions for the senior adults. As a group, the youth list important events from the last eighty to one hundred years—World War I, World War II, the Depression, the civil rights movement, etc. Then draw a timeline chart for the same period, labeling the chart in five-year increments (1900, 1905, 1910, etc.). Write the events on the timeline. You can also have both the youth and the senior adults identify the years they were born on the timeline. This timeline will provide a historical context for the interviews and help young people understand the temporal context of the senior adults' responses.

- **Collect old photos and memorabilia.** Ask participants to bring in old photos (of themselves, their families, and their communities), family mementos, and old newspaper articles that describe events highlighted in the "historical timeline" activity. These can be displayed, made into a collage, or organized on the historical timeline.

- **Discuss personal and social history.** Ask youth to consider questions such as "What happened last month? last year? five years ago? ten years ago?" This will help them develop a concrete awareness of actual, experienced life in a temporal context.

Activity 3B: Prepare the Interviews

The following activities will help prepare for the actual interviews:

- **Develop the interview questions.** Youth should work together in small groups to develop at least ten interview questions. There should be the same number of groups as the number of senior adults. The senior adults meet with each other to develop their own interview questions. If there is not enough time to work with the seniors, provide them with the sample questions on the facing page as a starting point.

- **Conduct interview training.** Youth and senior adults need to be oriented or reoriented to the principles of interviewing. This can be done by reviewing the list of interviewing skills presented on page 48 and conducting a series of interview role plays designed to highlight these principles. The Talk Show activity described on page 36 is a good example of a fun role-playing game that helps to develop interview skills.

- **Encourage senior adults to share their life stories.** The senior adults may need encouragement to share their life experiences. If that is the case, prompt them by reminding them: "Your life is and has been filled with fascinating experiences. I am sure the children will be very interested." Once they start to talk about their lives—and the young people start asking questions—they will probably find that they have a lot of interesting stories to share.

Two Dozen Questions For Senior Adults To Ask Young People

1.   What is your name?

2.   How old are you?

3.   Where were you born?

4.   How many people are in your family? How many brothers and sisters?
         Do you have grandparents and great-grandparents? What kinds of things do you do with them?

5.   What chores do you have to do around the house?

6.   What hobbies do you have?

7.   What do you like to read? (books, magazines, newspapers)

8.   What TV programs do you watch? Why do you like these programs?

9.   Do you have "best friends?" If so, how did they become your best friends?
         What kinds of things do you like to do with your friends or best friends?

10.   Do you go to a house of worship? If so, which one(s) do you go to?

11.   Is there anybody who you admire or think a lot of? Why?

12.   What kinds of clothes are in now?

13.   What kind of music is in now?

14.   What kinds of food do you like to eat? What are your least favorite foods?

15.   What do you like most about school? What do you like least? What would you like to change?

16.   What do you do after school?

17.   Is there anyone at home when you get there after school?

18.   What do you think about us coming to your class each week?

19.   What kinds of things do you think we might enjoy doing together outside of the classroom?

20.   Do you have any concerns about your neighborhood? If so, what are your biggest concerns?

21.   Are there enough things for you to do in your neighborhood for recreation?

22.   How do you think life will be for you when you get to be my age?

23.   What would you like the year 2000 (2010? 2020?) to be like?

24.   Is there anything that you would like to discuss with me? If so, what?

How to Interview People:
A Skills Checklist
developed by Bill Wertheim

✔ An interview is just like talking with someone, but with prepared questions. An interview helps us learn about someone or something.

✔ Remember: **Who? What? Where? When? Why? How?** Have a lot of good questions to ask. Develop at least one of each type of question.

✔ Being a little nervous is natural. Don't let it stop you.

✔ If you show someone that you care about what they are saying, they will want to continue talking. Everyone wants to be valued and listened to.

✔ **Listen as hard as you can**. After awhile, this will be easier. Be an active listener, a partner in the interview.

✔ Ask your questions slowly and give your partner time to answer.

✔ If someone says "I would rather not talk about that," that's okay. Some people want to be private about some things.

✔ Remember that when you are talking with someone, you are talking with them about their lives. Be respectful with all of the people you talk with and **always pay attention**.

Activity 3C: Conduct the Interviews

This activity concludes Unit 3:

- **Youth interview the senior adults.** After giving brief instructions about how to use the tape recorders, assign one senior adult to each group of young people. It will probably be necessary to provide ongoing encouragement to the youth to slow down their interviews and to ask follow-up questions. If possible, the program coordinator should meet with the senior volunteers to explore strategies for improving the young people's communication skills.

- **Senior adults interview the youth.** In the same groups as above, the senior adults conduct group interviews with the youth. The young people can provide group answers for each of the seniors' questions or take turns answering them.

Homework Ideas

- Distribute the "Interview Report Homework Assignment" provided at the end of this book (see "Worksheets and Handouts") to help young people think about the information gathered in the interviews.

  - Ask the youth participants to write about the interviews in their journals, particularly their feelings about the important issues that came up. Ask the senior volunteers to write journal entries also.

- Encourage the young people to practice their interview skills by interviewing their parents and grandparents, using the interview format developed for this activity.

Considerations

While this activity is valuable for helping youth develop their interviewing skills, it can also have a significant impact on program participants' values and attitudes regarding interpersonal and intergenerational communication, as illustrated by the following quotes:

"They interviewed me for sixty minutes . . . and when they asked me how old I was, they showed a big expression on their faces; they were so surprised at the age. I told them that I'll be 81 in August and I told them that I enjoy being with them."
—*Senior adult volunteer, Long Island City-2000*

"I didn't realize how lively they are . . . and how much they can talk about."
—*Fifth grade student (Royal Elementary School), Downtown-2000, Honolulu*

"Can you believe it? . . . They asked me 'Did they give out free condoms at hospitals when you were younger?' and I answered, 'Nothing was for free. Everybody was responsible for [taking care of] themselves.'"
—*Senior adult volunteer, Long Island City-2000*

UNIT 4: Land-Use Mapping

Objectives

- To familiarize participants with the distribution of land-use functions in their neighborhoods.

- To stimulate critical thought about what is missing or what should be changed in local neighborhoods.

- To provide a meaningful experience with maps for participants through the use of aerial photographs and the mapping of places relevant to their lives.

- To stimulate the exchange of information and the discovery of unknown places and features in the local environment.

Concepts and Skills

- **Concepts:** Analysis of the concepts of neighborhood and environment; uses of maps, including the display of different categories of phenomena in relation to geographical location and for making plans for the future by displaying existing spatial arrangements and a desired spatial arrangement at some future date.

- **Academic Skills Enhanced:** Various mathematical operations; resourcefulness with graphic arts materials; group communication skills; and the following mapping skills:

  — Review of fundamental map elements, including symbols, legends or map keys, scale, the use of grids for locating places, compass use/cardinal directions, titles, place names, and street indices.

  — Design of special use maps, including identification of categories to be used and design of map symbols (in this case, colors) to be employed in the maps.

  — Discovery of alternative sources of information for developing maps: personal knowledge and other published sources, such as interviews, aerial photos, and other types of maps.

Support Materials

- Copies of an outline map of the neighborhood (at least one copy per group). Each map should be large enough for at least four people to work on at once (when laid out it should occupy three to four desks joined together). There should be a group copy of this map on the wall in a location visible to everyone. Draw grid lines on this copy of the map at four-inch intervals and label them with numbers down the left side and letters across the top from left to right.

- At least one copy of a land-use map or aerial photograph of the neighborhood, which the groups can use to find the information they need. Such maps and photos can usually be obtained from local planning departments. These resources should be placed in a central location so that each group may carry them to its table as needed.

- Colored markers or colored pencils (one set of 10-12 colors per group)

  - Rulers (1-2 per group)

  - Compasses (ideally, 1 per group)

  - Colored stickers or push pins (1 per person)

  - Masking tape

Local land-use planners can be helpful resources for explaining the various types of maps and their uses.

Activity 4A: Orientation to the Map

- **Room and group organization.** Desks or tables should be organized into groups, ideally with four people per group—one senior and three youth. Each group should have an outline map, markers or colored pencils, and a ruler.

- **Orient the map.** If the room you are working in has windows, it might help some of the youth and senior adults to have their maps rotated into correct orientation with the landscape. If there is a north arrow marked on the map, the compass can be used to orient the map by simply placing it next to the north arrow and turning the map until it is correctly aligned with the north pointer of the compass. If there is no north arrow on the map, the group may line up landmarks viewed from the window with those same features on the map. They should also draw a north arrow in a blank area on the edge of the map.

- **Orientation to the map.** To start this activity, participants need to make a personal connection to the outline map. Following that, most of the remainder of the activity develops without much effort from the coordinators as the group members excitedly join in the game of identifying all the places in their neighborhood.

    Most large-scale outline neighborhood maps will have at least the major streets named, but little or nothing else may be marked. Choose a local landmark everyone knows and ask them to find it. This can be done in the form of a competition. Have someone come up and mark it on the copy of the map in front of the class.

    For the next landmark (perhaps the school or community center), have participants name the grid square in which it is located. This orientation exercise will review the use of grid lines as a map reference system.

    Also, ask participants to place colored stickers or push pins onto the map at the front of the class to show the location of their homes. Attach small pieces of masking tape to the back of each pin, number them, and make a chart listing each person's number.

Activity 4B: Mapping Land Uses

In this activity, small groups develop maps that identify the current land uses in their neighborhoods. These maps will be valuable tools for the remainder of the project, particularly for subsequent group discussions about future plans for the neighborhoods.

- **Name the map.** In a blank space on the edge of the map, have the youth write the title, "A Land-Use Map of _____."

- **Explain what a land-use map is.** Explain that in order for planners to plan for the future, they first need to know where things are in the present. For example, if they need to decide whether a new park or playground is needed and where to locate it, they look at the current pattern of residences in relation to the current distribution of green spaces in the neighborhood. Perhaps there is a large area of housing with no green space nearby, or perhaps there are abandoned lots with nothing on them at all. All of this information can be learned from a land-use map.

  A land-use map is made by coloring in all of the spaces on the map using different colors to show different uses, such as parks, houses, stores, and abandoned lots.

- **Develop the categories and symbols for the map.** Once the participants understand the purpose of the map, they should be able to suggest relevant categories. A list of these suggestions from the youth should be written on the blackboard, leading to a group discussion of the appropriateness of these categories for planning purposes. Colors should be discussed by the groups for each of these categories and agreed upon for uniformity on all maps. For example, groups usually choose green to represent parks and playgrounds. Explain to the students that after they begin they can suggest additional categories.

- **Complete the exercise.** To hasten completion of the exercise while stressing its collaborative nature, make each group responsible for just one area of the neighborhood. To this end, groups can be organized according to the location of participants' homes within the neighborhood.

Homework Ideas

- If after the first mapping session there are still some places unidentified, ask students to take home a photocopy of their section of the map to complete after doing field work observations on their own. They can also make a tracing or sketch map of the missing sections to take home. Ask them to determine the land-use functions of their sections (using the categories already developed) and color them in on the group map.

- Pick a block and write a paragraph about what is there now, what you think should be there instead, and why.

Considerations

Young people enjoy this mapping activity because it involves discovering and using a new medium and gives them a chance to demonstrate their considerable neighborhood knowledge. It is particularly useful, however, if a local planner can illustrate for them, with another area of the city, how important land-use maps are in the planning of future developments.

These activities can be reinforced through follow-up trips to social studies or city planning exhibits. Your local planning department should be able to help you locate such resources, either in their offices or at local museums or universities. For example, there is a three-dimensional model of New York City displayed at the Queens Museum in New York. There are similar models of Boston (at the Boston Redevelopment Agency), San Francisco (at the University of California-Berkeley's Environmental Simulation Lab), and most other large and medium-size cities.

If possible, use regional maps to illustrate the geographical relationship between the participants' neighborhood and the city, state, and/or region they live in.

Objectives

- To enhance participants' familiarity with local geography.

- To identify the range of places known, used, liked, and disliked by the youth and senior adults.

- To discover similarities and differences in perceptions of local places.

- To improve participants' map reading and observation skills in relation to the built environment.

Concepts and Skills

- **Concepts:** Community development and land use; how a city grows and uses its land; neighborhood; environmental transformation; expanded definition of geography.

- **Academic Skills Enhanced:** Tours can be easily linked to subjects in the school curriculum, including:

  — *History:* The historical significance of the tour can be brought out by highlighting recollections of senior adults that relate to various neighborhood sites, institutions, and patterns of living.

  — *Civics:* An examination of the role of government in community development—a typical focal point for local studies tours—will enhance participants' familiarity with city and state agencies dealing with employment, health and welfare, parks and recreation, police, fire, and sanitation. Also, through interviews with people who use or manage each organization or place visited on the tour, participants gain an awareness of how the physical environment constantly changes and how political decisions modify the local environment every day.

  — *Art:* Participants can become more aware of how the various forms, colors, patterns, and textures of elements in the environment relate to their visual and tactile senses in aesthetic as well as functional ways.

  — *Economics:* Emphasis should be placed on identifying which community locations are desirable and how this desirability affects land values and development.

— *Literature/Language Skills:* Aspects of the tour can be used to reinforce students' readings of literature (both fiction and non-fiction) about places or features of the environment. The increased awareness of local history and environmental meanings, and the need to clearly express this new knowledge, can lead to expanded verbal and writing skills.

— *Mathematics:* Emphasis can be placed on noting the simple geometric relationships of land use and real estate development; the financial cost-benefit analyses influencing the development of specific sites; and the precision measurement and mathematical calculations involved in building design and construction.

— *Science:* The walking tours will create opportunities to focus on how both natural processes and modern technology can modify environments, and opportunities to explore how ecological systems and the man-made environment influence each other.

Support Materials

- Parental Permission Form from each youth participant (see "Worksheets and Handouts")

- Large neighborhood map

- 2-4 cameras

- Black and white or color film

- Small outline maps of the neighborhood, 1 per participant

Activity 5A: Tour Preparation

There are a number of preparational tasks that should be completed prior to the tour:

- Obtain parental permission slips well in advance of the outing.

- Review the local map with the group.

- Discuss priorities, requirements, elements of interest, and other considerations for developing walking tour routes and emphases.

- Divide participants into groups based upon geographical considerations, such as the location of residences.

- In their groups, have participants discuss and develop their tours (one tour per group) with the assistance of interns.

- For each of the following categories, have each participant list two or more sites:

  — places you like

  — places you use by necessity

  — places with sentimental value

  — places you dislike

  — places you would like to learn more about

  — places you avoid

Ask youth to list places that are so important to them they think they will remember them when they grow up. Ask seniors to list places so important they recall them from their childhoods. In addition to formal institutions and places of relevance to their lives (such as the police precinct, library, local newspapers, and the community planning office—see the places listed in "Develop Community Connections" on pages 19 and 20), participants should be encouraged to identify informal places of meaning, such as corners, benches, and stoops. Keep in mind that some of the formal institutions, such as the local police precincts, will require advance permission to visit.

- If there are logistical problems with developing a series of mini-tours (with each group going on its own tour), hold a full-group meeting to develop one overall tour. Pinpoint selected locations on a large map and draw out a route that incorporates as many key sites as possible. Participants should copy the itinerary into their journals.

- If possible, practice the tour beforehand—perhaps a rehearsal conducted by the interns—to obtain a general idea of time and resources required, things encountered, and so on.

Activity 5B: Walk-About, Talk-About

In this part of the unit, participants go on the tour(s) they have planned:

- On the tours, participants should make extensive use of their journals, tape recorders, and cameras to record their observations, considerations, and discussions.

- Take time to carefully examine each organization and place visited. Encourage dialogue among the participants and between the participants and the various people they encounter during the tour.

- Try alternative walking tour methodologies. One interesting approach is a game in which participants pretend to be detectives searching for trace elements, environmental signs, or remnants of people's presence (wrappers, paths, graffiti, etc.).

Activity 5C: Tour Follow-Up

- As a large group, discuss the tours and what participants learned about each other, other neighborhood residents, and local development issues and needs. Focus on the evolution of local sites of interest and the multiple uses of each location.

Homework Ideas

- Imagine you are a stranger to this neighborhood (perhaps you are visiting from another country) and write a short poem or story about what you saw on the tour you just completed.

Considerations

The "Walk-About, Talk-About" activity is different from typical field trips in several ways. First, the youth and senior adults, not the group leader, do the majority of the planning for these tours. In addition, rather than passively viewing the sites, youth and seniors are actively engaged in observation and recording those observations. Emphasis should be placed on communication between the participants and the wider community.

Keep in mind that the tours can be useful for identifying previously untapped resource people and organizations in the community for involvement in other program activities, such as Display Day (see Unit 8, pages 70-72).

If your organization is planning field trips to other neighborhoods or cities, try to include meetings with local architects, transportation experts, sanitation experts, and other community planners who might help highlight interneighborhood and/or intercity comparisons.

UNIT 6: Community Interviews

Objectives

- To obtain information and recommendations from the community about specific sites and issues.

- To obtain feedback on participants' neighborhood improvement ideas.

Concepts and Skills

- **Concepts:** Community participation; how people influence each other; social responsibility.

- **Academic Skills Enhanced:** Development and execution of a structured interview; transcription and organization of material into coherent paragraphs; classification and/or categorization of, and drawing inferences from, interview data; development of constructive attitudes and sensitivity toward diversity, particularly in regard to community lives and the specific needs of different populations.

Support Materials

- 3-5 mini-tape recorders and tapes (optional)

Activity 6A: Prepare for the Interviews

- **Hold a group discussion.** A democratic selection process helps maintain participant interest in the data collection, analysis, and results presentations components of this activity. To begin this activity, a group meeting should be held to accomplish the following:

  — *Clarify issues.* As a full group, identify issues to be addressed. This discussion should begin with a review of the community issues and concerns identified in earlier activities, targeting those issues participants would like to explore more fully.

  — *Identify the interviewees.* Once the research topics are established, participants need to determine who to interview. Emphasis should be placed on obtaining a wide range of perspectives. For example, if participants decide to explore community safety issues, their sample might include: police officers; store owners; a cross-section of residents varying in age, gender, and physical ability; people who work but do not live in the neighborhood; and local civic organization staff.

- **Conduct interview training.** With assistance from the interns, organize and conduct a training session, including a review of interviewing skills (see page 48), highlights of what participants learned from the previous interviewing exercise (Unit 3), and an orientation to conducting interviews in the field.

- **Organize in small groups.** Small intergenerational groups should be formed to conduct the community interviews, with each group responsible for one or two interviews.

- **Develop interview questions.** Each group should develop the questions it will ask. The interviews should be brief, so seven to twelve questions should be sufficient. Interviews should include both open- and close-ended questions.

Activity 6B: Interview Community Members

Interviews of community members should be conducted by small intergenerational groups with an intern or program coordinator present. With proper planning, these groups can be mobilized on each field trip into the community. If time is limited, participants can conduct community interviews as part of their homework assignments. Group members can organize themselves so that one person is responsible for the tape recorder while others are responsible for taking notes or making sure that all of the planned questions are asked. Rehearsal and role-playing techniques can be used to help prepare for the interviews.

Activity 6C: Interview Follow-up

- **Analyze the results.** After the interviews are conducted, review the results as a full group and develop a categorization system based on the content of the responses. To do this:

  — List all of the responses given to each question.

  — Develop response categories that reflect the full range of responses (some responses may apply to more than one category—that's okay; enter them into all of the categories that apply).

  — Tabulate the numbers of responses fitting into each response category.

- **Develop a summary presentation.** A special committee of youth and senior adults can be chosen to develop and post a chart that clearly represents the interview results. This chart should also be shown at Display Day (see Unit 8, pages 70-72).

Homework Ideas

This entire unit—from determining research topics to analyzing data—can be conducted as a series of homework assignments.

Considerations

The community interviewing activity should be introduced in the context of questions raised by previous activities. It is an opportunity to further explore neighborhood concerns and issues as a collaborative learning process.

In preparing participants to conduct the interviews, encourage them to practice with their family members. Group role-playing activities can also be used to help reduce anxiety and to prepare participants for interviewing.

UNIT 7: Improving the Neighborhood

Objectives

- To stimulate participants to critically review neighborhood conditions.

- To give participants an opportunity to apply what they have learned in previous activities about neighborhood development issues.

- To develop specific recommendations for presentation to those involved in community development decision making. Presentation formats might include letters, Display Day (see Unit 8), and local media coverage.

Concepts and Skills

- **Concepts:** Citizen participation; contrasting viewpoints; belonging to a community.

- **Academic Skills Enhanced:** Group problem-solving strategies; summarization; preparation of graphic materials (maps, tables, diagrams, drawings); use of different media, including audio tapes and photography; cognitive integration of prior coursework; formulation of projections—hypothesizing change, assessing feasibility, and predicting the impact of proposed solutions; and development of constructive attitudes toward change and conflict.

Support Materials

- Large poster paper and cardboard for chartmaking.

Activity 7A: Develop and Evaluate Proposals

Based on historical accounts and the group's own investigation of current neighborhood conditions, participants are able to invent and evaluate alternative options for future development of their neighborhood. Following is a general procedure that can be used to generate proposals for the neighborhood as a whole, to develop solutions for certain "landmark" or problem sites, or to address particular issues of social concern.

- **Review neighborhood concerns and desires.** Organize a display of the information developed to date (maps, charts, models, tables, and summary lists of points about each issue) in the front of the room. Facilitate a group discussion to review the key neighborhood concerns and desires that have been identified.

- **Develop images of the community's past, present, and desired future.** Organize small groups based on residence, issues of interest, or randomly assigned study sites. Based on these assignments, each group should develop images highlighting aspects of their community's past, present, and desired future (sketches, photos, etc.). Integrate these images into one large chart divided into three parts—"Past," "Present," and "Future." If desired, participants can write slogans to go with certain images. This chart can serve as a stimulus for identifying the issues on which program participants choose to focus.

- **Develop and evaluate proposals.** List three column headings on the front blackboard or chart: "Recommendations," "Positive Impacts," and "Negative Impacts." Using the "desired futures" already identified as a starting point, list the group's recommendations for improving the neighborhood. Have participants point out the potential positive and negative impacts of each recommendation. At the end of this session, improve the three columns by pointing out inconsistencies, conflicts, and gaps in the ideas and information presented in them. For example, participants might note a potential conflict between their recommendation to build more houses for the homeless and their recommendation to limit new development projects. Refine the proposals to make them consistent.

■ **Identify key proposals.** By this point, the group should have a sense of the key issues and proposals they wish to highlight. Through democratic procedure, the group might choose to develop a scheme for one overall community development plan or to develop thematic presentations or exhibits for each locality or issue of concern. Examples of an issue-based approach would be for the group to focus its efforts on:

— Developing and publicizing solutions for wheelchair accessibility problems.

— Highlighting the unmet recreational needs of various groups in the community.

— Developing an anti-drug information campaign targeting school-aged children.

■ **Contact property owners.** If participants choose to put forth proposals for specific sites, they should contact the owner or manager of the property involved to find out about present and future plans before generating new ones.

Developing proposals for improving the neighborhood requires a careful review of existing conditions.

Activity 7B: Develop Presentations

Groups should determine the medium through which they will present their concerns and proposals for neighborhood improvement, such as photographs, maps, sketches, models, charts, songs, skits, dances, and video. Among the many ways in which program participants can express their ideas for neighborhood improvement are:

- Letter-writing campaigns to newspapers defining and suggesting solutions to one or more local problems.

- Presenting skits developed to highlight specific problems.

- Making photo-based collages. This procedure, developed by Ray Lorenzo for evoking ideas and proposals for neighborhood change, involves developing collages of desired future images, beginning with photographs of sites of interest. It can work with slide film, black and white photos, and copies of photos. See Hart and Moore (1982-1983).

- Exhibiting murals, models, and charts developed during activities at community meetings and fairs.

- Conducting sit-ins, demonstrations, or boycotts as a strategy for restoring civil rights that might have been violated. Group discussion could also include a review of the civil rights movement of the 1960s.

For additional ideas for community action projects, refer to the *Training Student Organizers Curriculum (Revised Edition)* by Zamm, Ortner, and DeAngelis (1990), or the Close Up Foundation publication entitled *Building Bridges To Citizenship: How To Create Successful Intergenerational Citizenship Programs* (1989).

Homework Ideas

- Draw a picture of a building from the past, and then modify it for the future.

- Draw a picture of a new building in your neighborhood, and then modify it so it looks like it existed in the past.

Considerations

This is the least-defined activity of this curriculum insofar as it is hard to know the size and complexity of the community problems to be addressed by each program until this phase is reached.

It is very easy to become absorbed in either the historical or present aspects of life in a neighborhood and to neglect study of the future. It is important that the group leaders encourage participants to focus on the future. The ability to visualize, anticipate, and plan for change should not be taken for granted.

To maximize the participants' potential for facilitating neighborhood improvement, emphasis should be placed on selecting issues of concern to the larger community, such as crime, unemployment, drug abuse, graffiti, or pedestrian safety. Interviews with family members might provide additional insights into neighborhood issues and the potential for action.

The primary goal is to develop specific recommendations for action, as opposed to vague statements about what "needs to be done." Yet despite the locations or issues chosen, it is important to emphasize to participants from the start of the program that there will not necessarily be any direct action resulting from their efforts. Nevertheless, if they present a broad range of possible alternative futures for their community environment, including the potential effects of taking no action at all, they can make a useful contribution to a better understanding of community issues.

UNIT 8: Display Day

Objectives

- To enable participants to present their alternative neighborhood plans to other community residents, the local press, and those individuals in neighborhood, city, state, and federal agencies responsible for making local planning decisions.

- To develop an understanding of local development decision-making processes and the people who help make such decisions.

Concepts and Skills

- **Concepts:** Synthesis of information learned in activities; teaching others the neighborhood's history and future possibilities; community development decisions as the result of a democratic process.

- **Academic Skills Enhanced:** Strategies for finding out about community development issues; sharpened descriptive, observational, perceptive, and graphic skills; photography, model making, and map-reading skills; use of media and visual displays for communicating ideas.

Support Materials

- Enough copies of an end-of-year booklet (see Activity 8A) for everyone who will be attending Display Day.

- Refreshments for participants and visitors.

Activity 8A: Plan and Prepare for the Event

In this phase, participants organize a special event, open to the community, to display the findings and proposals resulting from their research and activities.

- **Develop a program summary booklet.** In addition to the photographs, maps, sketches, models, and collages on display, people attending this event should receive a booklet summarizing the program's activities and resulting proposals. The booklet should incorporate program participants' written and pictorial accounts of their investigation of specific locations, organizations, and/or issues throughout the program.

- **Organize the event and the displays.** In addition to the final proposals, have different groups of young people and senior adults be responsible for organizing displays to summarize the various activities that were undertaken in the program and the outcome of each. Have at least one group be responsible for refreshments and decorations for the event. You can also establish a publicity committee to help ensure that the event is widely announced.

- **Announce the event.** Create formal invitations and flyers and distribute them around the neighborhood to publicize the event. Make participants aware that their decisions about who to invite will affect the chances for promoting their neighborhood improvement recommendations. It is important, for example, to invite representatives from city agencies and community organizations who make local development decisions or who otherwise influence the quality of community life.

Activity 8B: Hold the Event

The Display Day event is an opportunity for participants to have fun and be proud of their accomplishments. Every event will have its own character and atmosphere. Some will be quite formal, whereas others will be very informal. Either way, be sure that the event includes a mechanism to allow program participants to receive feedback from the residents, planners, politicians, and citizen advisory group representatives who attend. This could be a simple questionnaire with two to four questions or simply a general discussion following presentation of the group's proposals.

Display Day provides program participants with an opportunity to reflect on their community development ideas and proposals.

Homework Ideas

- Make a list of ways to publicize the event through newspapers, radio, and flyers, and then enact your ideas.

- Design a flyer, a logo, and invitations to attract people to Display Day.

- Distribute flyers and invitations.

- Develop substantive questions for the community residents, local development organization administrators, and politicians attending the event.

Considerations

Display Day is the culmination of the program. It is the point where participants share the results of their community investigations, their concerns about neighborhood problems, and their ideas for improving neighborhood conditions. It is their chance to present their ideas to an interested audience.

To enhance the program's impact, it is a good idea to invite other program groups or classes to attend the event. Also, to recruit senior adult volunteers for subsequent programs, it is useful to invite senior adults from the local senior centers to which participating volunteers belong, as well as senior groups from local churches and synagogues.

If possible, document the event with photographs and videotape.

UNIT 9: Concluding Meeting

Objectives

- To obtain written and verbal feedback on the program from the participants.

- To enable participants to attain emotional closure in the new relationships they have formed.

Concepts and Skills

- **Concepts:** Program evaluation; interdependence; common citizenship.

- **Academic Skills Enhanced:** Critical thinking; problem solving; articulation of ideas; interpersonal and group relations.

Support Materials

- Refreshments for the program participants (optional).

Activity

The group reviews the presentations made at Display Day and discusses how people responded to their suggestions. If time permits, this meeting can begin with a presentation by a local planner or community development agency representative about current city planning efforts, followed by a period for dialogue with participants.

The most important aspect of this meeting is for the group to discuss the program. What was good about the curriculum? What could be made better? Did the seniors get as much from it as the youth? The program coordinator should include this information in the final weekly log sheet (provided at the end of the book under "Worksheets and Handouts").

In addition, encourage the group to discuss what they learned about each other. Have their perceptions about young people or seniors changed?

Homework Ideas

- For group discussion, write about three things you would change to make this program better.

- Complete the post-program questionnaire (see "Worksheets and Handouts").

Considerations

Since this final meeting could mark the end of the intergenerational relationships participants developed, it should provide emotional closure and/or promote future interaction.

Additional Activity Ideas

Additional Activity Ideas

The activities presented in the nine program units on the preceding pages provide a framework which can be easily modified and enhanced. Program organizers are encouraged to improvise and develop new activities to utilize each group's special strengths and respond to each group's particular needs. Following are some guidelines and ideas for developing additional activities. An excellent reference for additional intergenerational activity ideas is *Growing Together: An Intergenerational Sourcebook*, edited by Strunz and Reville (1985).

- **Develop Activities Based on the Group's Strengths and Uniqueness.** Every group will have unique characteristics that offer programming possibilities. For example, a culturally diverse group might develop dance and food exchange activities based on the diversity of the group members. If a group has some Latino seniors who enjoy salsa dancing, ask them teach it to the youth. Better yet, organize a "Dance Down" event where youth and seniors teach their dances to each other. While you should avoid facilitating intergenerational competition, a slight competitive thrust (who can learn the other group's dances quicker or better?) might provide participants with the initial motivation to learn each other's dances.

- **Develop Activities Based on School Subjects and Assignments.** The general curriculum of the school or youth program is an excellent source of activity ideas. Activities that are developed to tie in with other school work reinforce *Side by Side*'s educational value and can help enliven other curriculum subjects.

A good example was developed by Bill Wertheim for the *Mt. Vernon–2000* program. It is a poetry writing exercise designed to teach youth how to understand and write poetry while working with senior adults and learning to appreciate their experiences. In this activity, program leaders distribute a poem that provides a rich description of a person's experience with a place. Participants then discuss the poem, responding to questions such as "What is this a picture of?," "How does the writer feel about this place?," and other questions that encourage critical thought about the poem and descriptive writing in general. Participants can also suggest titles for the poem based on the places they know that are like that (e.g., "Brooklyn in Spring," "A Road in the Desert," etc.). Each participant then writes their own poem about a place they have lived or visited, describing the colors, smells, sounds, and images of that place.

- **Develop Activities That Draw on Aspects of Daily Living.** Any aspect of community life can be readily transposed into an exciting intergenerational activity. For example, the topic of "what people wear" can lead to a hat show or fashion show through which youth and senior adult participants share their dressing styles, an important aspect of themselves. "What people say" can be explored through the creation of a slang chart that compares slang expressions used by the youth, adults, and senior adults. "What people do for fun" can lead to a community interviewing activity similar to the one presented in Unit 5. These and similar activity ideas are listed below:

This Aspect of Daily Life	*can be explored through*	This Type of Activity
What people wear		hat or fashion show
What people say		chart of slang terms
What people like to do		"dance down" competition *or* "share your favorite hobby" activity *or* comparison of old and new games
Social and family values		list "the commandments of good living" *or* list things that are "right" and "wrong"
The need for self expression		intergenerational poetry writing
Curiosity about community life		community interviewing *or* video documentation of local activities, street life, etc.

The Commandments of Good Living

This activity evolved from the interests of group members in a program in Mount Vernon in 1990. The catalyst for the activity was a senior volunteer's intense concern about the moral development of today's youth. He brought in a list of seven "Rules to Live By" derived from the Bible's Ten Commandments. His initial intention was to have the students study and share these rules with their families. From this initiative, the group developed a collaborative exercise in which the students and senior adults discussed each of these rules and created additional ones, resulting in the 22 "Commandments of Good Living" (listed at right). The activity helped to clarify group values and (through presentation at Display Day) to stimulate reflection and dialogue about social and family values among a much larger group of community members.

1. No self-destruction (stealing, killing one another).
2. Live freely.
3. There should be no lying.
4. Let everybody in the family be proud of you.
5. Parents shouldn't yell when a child does something wrong, and also should be less protective when it isn't necessary.
6. Treat others the way you want them to treat you.
7. Listen to what kids are saying to you.
8. Kids should not ignore adults.
9. Don't commit adultery.
10. There should be no rape.
11. People should not use drugs.
12. Parents shall respect their children.
13. There should be more love and peace in the world.
14. No one should smoke cigarettes.
15. No lighting matches when no one is at home.
16. Love yourself, care for yourself, discipline yourself, and respect yourself. Love and care for the family and for all people.
17. Everyone should have a fair share of the world's resources.
18. No cursing at one's parents.
19. Respect others.
20. Respect parents no matter what.
21. There should be no cursing.
22. You should have the freedom to speak to your parents about yourself without fear.

- **Develop Activities That Connect Students with the Community.** Every community will have unique resources that can provide the basis for *Side by Side* activities. These resources might include community leaders, local businesses, or special programs and institutions (e.g., a children's museum, art center, etc.). Both students and senior adults enjoy the opportunity to meet with local leaders or look "behind-the-scenes" at a well-known local business or institution. Most people in the community will welcome the opportunity to meet with young people and senior adults from their area and share their thoughts on the neighborhood and the role they play in it.

In the program in Mt. Vernon, NY, students and senior adults met with Mayor Ronald A. Blackwood to discuss city problems and possible solutions. (1989)

Program Assessment

E valuation of the program's process and outcomes is the final—and essential—step in any *Side by Side* program. It is easy to overlook or ignore the post-program evaluation. Don't. Take the time to conduct a complete and worthwhile evaluation to identify your program's strengths, weaknesses, and opportunities for improvement. The information you gather will be extremely valuable for future *Side by Side* programs, other intergenerational endeavors, programs in which similar situations or activities arise.

A number of criteria can be used to evaluate the success of a *Side by Side* program. Each program will need to identify its own criteria based on the specific goals and purposes of the program. Following are some general criteria that apply:

- Did it increase awareness of age-related stereotypes?

- Did it enhance understanding and cooperation between participating youth and senior adults?

- Did it improve understanding and appreciation of the local environment?

- Did it contribute to a greater understanding of human relatedness to the environment and development of values and ethics that suggest an enhanced sense of citizen responsibility?

Evaluation Tools

There are a number of evaluation tools and information sources that can be used to determine how well your program performed in relation to the identified evaluation criteria:

- **Journals and Other Documentation.** The program journals kept by participants may be the most valuable information sources for your program evaluation, providing a useful chronological indicator of the program's effectiveness. Also, throughout the program, group leaders (ideally, college interns) should carefully monitor and document the participation of youth and senior adult volunteers. Emphasis should be placed on logging intergenerational communication and those comments and actions related to participants' knowledge of and concerns about the neighborhood.

- **Questionnaires.** Administered before and after the program, questionnaires can be used to help gauge the program's impact on participants' knowledge of and attitudes toward people in other generations, as well as toward community affairs. Sample pre- and post-program questionnaires are provided in the appendix. These questionnaires should be shortened to incorporate only those items that are a priority to program organizers as it may be difficult to convince young people to fill out a long questionnaire.

- **Weekly Log Sheets.** Another important evaluation tool is the log sheet that group leaders may fill out on a weekly basis (see appendix). This can be used to clarify scheduling, curriculum integration, budgeting, staffing, and administrative considerations associated with each activity and the program as a whole.

- **Informal Feedback.** This is often the most valuable means of evaluating the program's effectiveness. Try to compare the comments participants make early in the program to those they make toward the end. Have their views changed toward intergenerational interaction? Community activism? Citizen responsibility? Are there any comments that reflect academic growth or communication skills development?

Words From the Wise

The following quotes illustrate the type of feedback that has come from teachers and students who have participated in programs based on the *Side by Side* model:

The attention that the senior citizens gave to the children made them feel special. That extra help and caring is what every child needs to gain confidence. It is something that one teacher in a classroom with many children cannot always accomplish.
—Fourth grade teacher (Washington Elementary School), Mount Vernon, NY

I was very impressed with the children's awareness of neighborhood problems and their understanding of the underlying causes, such as drugs. The program seems to be helping them focus on the entire neighborhood and understand the needs of the community as a whole. I was very proud of the actual presentations. The children spoke very well, presented their positions clearly and in logical sequence. This was done without rehearsal.
—Sixth grade teacher (P. S. 76), Long Island City, NY

The program is a life-line to kids who need to get to know someone who is older; someone to share thoughts with and most importantly, someone who cares about them . . . . Several students really enjoyed the seniors' company. It was becoming a centerpiece for them to share their thoughts with an older person in their family—a grandmother, aunt, or a grandfather.
—Fourth grade teacher (Washington Elementary School), Mount Vernon, NY

I learned that the city council has to agree [about neighborhood plans] before decisions are made.
—Fifth grade student (Royal Elementary School), Honolulu, HI

Well, otherwise [if we do not speak to older adults], how are we gonna relive the magic yesteryears? . . . If you don't have a history book, a senior citizen will do the job.
—Sixth grade student (P. S. 76), Long Island City, NY

A Final Note

This program model is not a fixed product. It will be continually expanded and modified according to feedback from teachers and community center staff who implement *Side by Side* programs. To promote information exchange between program sites, staff are encouraged to contact the author to share program evaluation data and new programming ideas. Information, ideas, feedback, and other inquiries may be sent to:

Matthew Kaplan
c/o MIG Communications
1802 Fifth Street
Berkeley, CA 94710

Appendices

Leaders in the intergenerational field and key organizations to contact for more information:

Center for Intergenerational Learning
Temple University
206 University Services Building
1601 North Broad Street
Philadelphia, PA 19122
phone 215/204-6970
fax 215/204-6733

Center for Understanding Aging
200 Executive Boulevard, Suite 201
P.O. Box 246
Southington, CT 06489-0246
phone 203/621-2079
fax 203/621-2989

Elders Share the Arts, Inc.
57 Willoughby Street
Brooklyn, NY 11201
phone 718/488-8565
fax 718/488-8296

Generations Together
University Center for Social and Urban Research
University of Pittsburgh
121 University Place, Suite 300
Pittsburgh, PA 15260
phone 412/648-7150
fax 412/624-4810

For more information about state and local intergenerational programming networks and for an update on national legislation initiatives that promote intergenerational programs and policies, contact:

Generations United
c/o Child Welfare League of America
440 First Street, NW, Suite 310
Washington, DC 20001-2085
phone 202/638-2952
fax 202/638-4004

For more information about intergenerational program initiatives and policies in New York State:

The New York State Intergenerational Network
Attention: Kevin Brabazon
New York City Department for the Aging
2 Lafayette Street, Fifteenth Floor
New York, NY 10007-1392
phone 212/442-1081
fax 212/442-1135

Baldassari, C., S. Lehman, and M. Wolfe. 1987. Imaging and creating alternative environments with children. In *Spaces for children: The built environment and child development*, T. David and C. Weinstein (eds.). New York: Plenum Press.

Close Up Foundation. 1989. *Building bridges to citizenship: How to create successful intergenerational citizenship programs.* Arlington, VA: Close Up Foundation.

Generations Together. 1986. *The Best of You . . . The Best of Me.* Pittsburgh, PA: University Center for Social and Urban Research, University of Pittsburgh. Video. [Can be rented or purchased; see address on page 89.]

Hart, R. 1987. Children's participation in planning and design: Theory, research and practice. In *Spaces for children: The built environment and child development*, C. Weinstein and T. David (eds.). New York: Plenum Press.

Hart, R. and R. Moore. 1982-1983. Participation 3: Techniques. *Childhood City Quarterly*, Vol. 9, Issues 1 and 4.

Kaplan, M. 1993. Recruiting senior adults for intergenerational programs: Working to create a jump on the bandwagon effect. *Journal of Applied Gerontology*, March issue.

Kaplan, M. 1991. *An intergenerational approach to community education and action.* Ph.D. dissertation. City University of New York Graduate Center.

Kaplan, M. 1990. Designing community participation special events that cross generational boundaries. In *Proceedings of the Twenty-First Annual Conference of the Environmental Design Research Association*, R. Selby, K. Anthony, J. Choi, and B. Orland (eds.). Champaign, IL: Environmental Design Research Association.

Kingson, Hirshorn, and Cornman. 1986. *Ties that bind: The interdependence of generations.* The Gerontological Society of America. York, PA: Maple Press Company.

Moody, H. and R. Disch. 1989. Intergenerational programming between young and old. *The Generational Journal*, 1 (3); 25-27.

Newman, S. and S. Brummel (eds.). 1989. *Intergenerational programs: Imperatives, strategies, impacts, trends.* Binghamton, NY: Haworth Press.

Seefeldt, C. 1987. Intergenerational programs: Making them work. *Journal of the Association for Childhood Education International*, October: 14-18.

Strunz, K. and S. Reville (eds.). 1985. *Growing together: An intergenerational sourcebook.* Jointly published by the American Association of Retired Persons and The Elvirita Lewis Foundation.

Stuen, C. et al. 1982. *Seniors teaching seniors: A manual for training older adult teachers.* New York: Institute on Aging, Columbia University School of Social Work.

Thorp, K. (ed.). 1985. *Intergenerational programs: A resource for community renewal.* Madison, WI: Wisconsin Positive Youth Development Initiative, Inc.

Ward, C. and A. Fyson. 1973. *Streetwork: The exploding school.* Boston, MA: Routledge and Kegan Paul.

Wilson, J. 1992. *Intergenerational readings 1980-1992: A bibliography of books, journal articles, manuals, papers, curricula, bibliographies, directories, newsletters, data bases, and videos.* Pittsburgh, PA: Generations Together, University of Pittsburgh. [Available for $17.50; see address on page 89.]

Zamm, M., R. Ortner, and B. DeAngelis. 1990. *Training student organizers curriculum*, Revised Edition. New York: Council on the Environment of New York City (51 Chambers Street, Room 228, New York, NY 10007; phone 212/566-0990).

Worksheets and Handouts

The following pages contain handouts and worksheets for use in conducting *Side by Side* program activities. They have been designed to be easily photocopied and distributed for use by program participants. However, you may wish to customize some forms based on the particular requirements of your program.

The handouts and worksheets included in this section are listed below, with page references to identify the location of the relevant activity description in this book:

- **My Journal and Me** *(page 30)*

- **Getting to Know You** *(page 31)*

- **Interview Report Homework Assignment** *(page 49)*

- **Parental Permission Form** *(pages 56-57)*

- **Weekly Log Sheet** *(page 84)*

- **Pre-Program Questionnaire** *(page 84)*

- **Post-Program Questionnaire** *(page 84)*

My Journal and Me

An Approach to Journal Writing

Developed by Kim Blakely and Bill Wertheim

Throughout this program, you will be asked to make a few notes, every day, about your experiences with older or younger people, your community, and yourself. You can write about all sorts of things, as long as the starting point is this program. In your journal, you are the boss.

It might be useful to keep the following things in mind:

1   My journal contains my thoughts and feelings about the program, and that is important. It is a home for my experiences during the time I am involved in the program.

2   My journal is my friend and keeps all secrets.

3   My journal is a place where I can say anything I feel. I don't have to say or do anything in my journal unless I want to.

4   My journal never yells back at me. I can say or do no wrong in my journal.

5   My journal helps me remember the things we have done in the program, what I have learned, and how I feel about the program.

6   I can write in this journal, draw in it, or cut out pictures of places and people or newspaper articles. I can interview people and write about them. My journal has everything I put into it, and it does not have the things that I don't put into it.

7   If I want to, I might talk about some of the ideas in my journal in class and with my family, friends, and the professionals who help plan and run my community.

8   Only I give permission for people to see my journal.

Getting to Know You

Interviewer's Name: _____

Interviewee's Name: _____

1   Do you have any family members or friends my age? If yes, who? What kinds of things do you usually do with them?

2   Where would you like to be living ten years from now? Why?

3   If your neighborhood has a name, what do you call it? If you could change two things about your neighborhood, what would they be?

4   Tell me two things you would like to learn or accomplish this year.

5   Do you think this neighborhood is getting better or worse? Why do you feel this way?

6   Is there anything else about yourself or your neighborhood that you would like to share with me?

Interview Report Homework Assignment

Write a report (one or two pages) on how things have changed over the past thirty to seventy years. Think about what you learned from interviewing the senior adult who was in your group.

To help you remember what you found out, we are giving you a tape recording of your interview. If you do not have a tape recorder or know somebody who has one that you can borrow, just review your notes from the interview. A tape recorder is not necessary for this exercise.

In your report, write about changes that have taken place, dealing with one of the following topics.

1 **School.** Has school changed? In what ways? What about homework responsibilities? What about dress?

2 **Family.** Are families different today? Did you grow up with your parents? What things did you do together?

3 **Recreation.** What did people do for fun? Do people have fun today in the same ways that they used to?

4 **Fashion.** What did people wear and how did they look? Do people dress any differently now than they used to? In what ways?

5 **Childhood.** What is different about growing up today than it was thirty to seventy years ago?

6 **Religion.** How is going to religious services today different from the past? How is it the same?

7 **Other Topics.** If you wish, you can choose your own topic to write about as long as you compare the past to the present.

To help you in writing your reports, speak to family members, your local librarian, and others who should be able to provide you with local history information.

Parental Permission Form

_____, 19___

Dear Parent,

Your child and others at _____ (name of school or organization) are participating in a new program called _____.
As part of this program, your child will be exploring the local neighborhood—as it was, as it is, and as it might be in the future. He or she will be working closely with a group of senior adult volunteers from the neighborhood.

We are requesting permission for your child to be included in **photographs** and **videotape** that may be taken of this program. These materials will be used to publicize the program in local papers and to document program activities. Please note that photography and videotaping of the program will be conducted with the assistance of participating youth and senior adult volunteers.

We would appreciate your consideration of our request for your consent. Please fill out the bottom of this form and give it to your child to return to us for our files. If you have any questions, please contact _____ at _____ (phone number).

Sincerely,

_____

Permission Statement

I, _____(parent's name), grant permission for my child to be included in photographs and videotape footage taken during the _____ program.

_____
Signature

Weekly Log Sheet

activities conducted this week	level of youth interest and involvement	dynamics between youth and senior adults	connections between program and curriculum

How might you suggest changing these activities to make them more educational and more conducive to promoting youth and senior adult community involvement?

Pre-Program Questionnaire

Name _____

Date _____

Place of Birth _____

Current Address _____

Telephone Number _____

How old are you? Circle the appropriate age category:

8-14   15-59   60-69   70-79   80-89   90+

Section A: Some Thoughts About Your Neighborhood

1   What do you call your neighborhood? (How do you refer to it?)

2   How long have you lived where you live now?

3   If you lived in another place before moving here, where did you live?

4   Do you have any relatives living in this neighborhood? If yes, how many?

5   **(a)**   What do you like about your neighborhood?

        (b)   What do you dislike about your neighborhood?

        (c)   What words would you use to describe life in your neighborhood?

6   Do you think there is anything in your neighborhood that should be changed?
Yes _____   No _____

If yes, what kinds of changes would you like to see?

7   What do you think residents care most about in your neighborhood?

8   **(a)**   Is there enough for you to do in your neighborhood?

           (b)   How do you spend most of your time?

           (c)   Are there any things you would like to do in your neighborhood but cannot?
                     Yes _____   No _____

           (d)   Please explain your answer to (c) above.

9   What else do you think there should be in your neighborhood? What kind of new places or things would you like to have?

10   Who do you think is responsible for deciding what will be built or changed in your community?

11   Are there any neighborhood improvement activities in which you would like to get involved?
Yes _____   No_____

If yes, what are they? If no, why not?

Section B: Some Thoughts About Young People/Senior Adults

For students, the following questions are about your attitudes toward senior adults (60 years of age or older). For senior adults, the following questions are about your attitudes toward young people (13 years of age or younger).

12   How often do you have conversations with senior adults or young people?

__ Never
__ Once a month or less
__ Once a week or less
__ 2-3 times a week
__ More than 3 times a week

13   In general, how do you feel about senior adults/youth?

14   Why do you think you feel this way?

15   How important do you think it is for young people and seniors to speak to each other?

__ Very Important
__ Important
__ Not Important but not Unimportant
__ Not Important
__ Very Unimportant

Please explain your answer.

16   Do you think you have anything to offer senior adults/youth?
Yes____   No____

If yes, what? If no, why not?

17   Do senior adults/youth have anything to offer you?
Yes ____   No ____

If yes, what? If no, why not?

18   For the following statements, circle the appropriate number to indicate whether you:

1   Strongly Agree
2   Agree
3   Neither Agree nor Disagree
4   Disagree
5   Strongly Disagree

1 2 3 4 5
Generally speaking, most seniors/young people are trustworthy.

1 2 3 4 5
Most seniors/young people try to be helpful.

1 2 3 4 5
Most seniors/young people try to be fair.

1 2 3 4 5
You can't be too careful in dealing with seniors/young people.

1 2 3 4 5
Most seniors/young people are just looking out for themselves.

1 2 3 4 5
Most seniors/young people would try to take advantage of you if they got the chance.

1 2 3 4 5
Most seniors/young people do not understand senior citizens and their needs.

1 2 3 4 5
Most seniors/young people do not care about improving the neighborhoods in which they live.

1 2 3 4 5
There are situations in which young people and seniors can work together.

19 Do you have any special skills or interests, such as photography, crafts, or dancing?

For senior adults only:

20 Do you have any experience working with young people in a school, a community center, or in a religious institution?
Yes ____   No ____

If so, please describe what you did.

21 From which of the following sources do you learn about young people?

___a. television   ___e. your children
___b. your grandchildren   ___f. neighbors
___c. your friends   ___g. from movies
___d. books   ___h. somewhere else (where?) _____

22 What words would you use to describe young people?

Post-Program Questionnaire

Name _____

Date _____

Place of Birth _____

Current Address _____

Telephone Number _____

How old are you? Circle the appropriate age category:

8-14   15-59   60-69   70-79   80-89   90+

Section A: Some Thoughts About Your Neighborhood

1   What do you call your neighborhood? (How do you refer to it?)

2   How long have you lived where you live now?

3   If you lived in another place before moving here, where did you live?

4   Do you have any relatives living in this neighborhood? If yes, how many?

5   **(a)**   What do you like about your neighborhood?

         (b)   What do you dislike about your neighborhood?

         (c)   What words would you use to describe life in your neighborhood?

6   Do you think there is anything in your neighborhood that should be changed?
Yes ____   No ____

If yes, what kinds of changes would you like to see?

7   What do you think residents care most about in your neighborhood?

8   **(a)**   Is there enough for you to do in your neighborhood?

        (b)   How do you spend most of your time?

        (c)   Are there any things you would like to do in your neighborhood but cannot?
                Yes ____   No ____

        (d)   Please explain your answer to (c) above.

9   What else do you think there should be in your neighborhood? What kind of new places or things would you like to have?

10   Who do you think is responsible for deciding what will be built or changed in your community?

11   Are there any neighborhood improvement activities in which you would like to get involved?
Yes ____   No____

If yes, what are they? If no, why not?

Section B: Some Thoughts About Young People/Senior Adults

For students, the following questions are about your attitudes toward senior adults (60 years of age or older). For senior adults, the following questions are about your attitudes toward young people (13 years of age or younger).

12 How often do you have conversations with senior adults or young people?

___ Never
___ Once a month or less
___ Once a week or less
___ 2-3 times a week
___ More than 3 times a week

13 In general, how do you feel about senior adults/youth?

14 Why do you think you feel this way?

15 How important do you think it is for young people and seniors to speak to each other?

___ Very Important
___ Important
___ Not Important but not Unimportant
___ Not Important
___ Very Unimportant

Please explain your answer.

16 Do you think you have anything to offer senior adults/youth?
Yes____   No____

If yes, what? If no, why not?

17 Do senior adults/youth have anything to offer you?
Yes ____   No ____

If yes, what? If no, why not?

18 For the following statements, circle the appropriate number to indicate whether you:

1 Strongly Agree
2 Agree
3 Neither Agree nor Disagree
4 Disagree
5 Strongly Disagree

1 2 3 4 5
Generally speaking, most seniors/young people are trustworthy.

1 2 3 4 5
Most seniors/young people try to be helpful.

1 2 3 4 5
Most seniors/young people try to be fair.

1 2 3 4 5
You can't be too careful in dealing with seniors/young people.

1 2 3 4 5
Most seniors/young people are just looking out for themselves.

1 2 3 4 5
Most seniors/young people would try to take advantage of you if they got the chance.

1 2 3 4 5
Most seniors/young people do not understand senior citizens and their needs.

1 2 3 4 5
Most seniors/young people do not care about improving the neighborhoods in which they live.

1 2 3 4 5
There are situations in which young people and seniors can work together.

19 Do you have any special skills or interests, such as photography, crafts, or dancing?

For senior adults only:

20 Do you have any experience working with young people in a school, a community center, or in a religious institution?
Yes _____   No _____

If so, please describe what you did.

21 From which of the following sources do you learn about young people?

___a. television   ___e. your children
___b. your grandchildren   ___f. neighbors
___c. your friends   ___g. from movies
___d. books   ___h. somewhere else (where?) _____

22 What words would you use to describe young people?

Section C: Some Thoughts About This Program
The following questions ask you to describe how you felt about participating in this program.

23 Did you learn anything about your neighborhood from this program? If yes, what?

How do you think we could have changed the program to make it more educational?

How do you think we could have changed the program to make it more fun?

24 Has this program given you any ideas about things you can do to improve your neighborhood? If yes, what?

25 Did you learn anything about how decisions are made which affect you and your neighborhood? If yes, what?

26 Have you changed your ideas about senior citizens as a result of working with them on this program? If yes, in what ways?

27 Did you feel differently about working with the senior citizen volunteers than you would have felt working with younger adult volunteers? Please explain.

28   How many class sessions have you missed? (If not sure, give an estimate): _____

29   In this program, you participated in seven types of program activities. Please number these activities according to how much you enjoyed them. Rank the activities from **1** to **8**. Use **1** for the activity you enjoyed the most, **2** for the activity you enjoyed the second best, and so on.

_____Model Building   _____Interviewing Senior Adults/Youth

_____Land-Use Mapping   _____Autobiographical Tours

_____Community Interviewing   _____Developing Neighborhood Improvement Ideas

_____Your Group's Final Project   _____Display Day Event

30   Please number the following activities according to how much you learned from them. Use **1** for the activity from which you learned the most, **2** for the activity from which you learned the second most, and so on.

_____Model Building   _____Interviewing Senior Adults/Youth

_____Land-Use Mapping   _____Autobiographical Tours

_____Community Interviewing   _____Developing Neighborhood Improvement Ideas

_____Your Group's Final Project   _____Display Day Event

31   Overall, how did you feel about participating in this program? Write a few sentences that convey a real feeling of what you thought about the program.

Notes